Thinking
Through Philosophy
Book 2

Written by
PAUL CLEGHORN

Stories by
STEPHANIE BAUDET

First Published
April 03 in Great Britain by

PUBLISHING

A CIP record for this work is available from the British Library

ISBN-10: 1-904374-41-7
ISBN-13: 978-1-904374-41-1

Typeset by Educational Printing Services Limited

E-mail: enquiries@eprint.co.uk   Website: www.eprint.co.uk

Thinking Through Philosophy

The development of 'thinking skills' has been identified as of great importance to the educational development of young people. Information handling, reasoning, creative thinking, and evaluation are all of great importance - and will be even more so as we move more and more towards a knowledge-based economy. How to think well will greatly affect a person's life chances! The other big influence on this is the emotional intelligence of the individual - are they self-aware, self-regulated, motivated, empathetic?

The 'Thinking Through Philosophy' programme develops both these important areas and is backed by current research. The book contains a 'theoretical' section that gives details of all facets of the programme, and a practical section containing thirty fully-detailed sessions, which comprise a year's work. No further planning is necessary.

This book (Book 2) is suitable for Years 4/5 and Years P5/6 (Scotland). The complete programme is a coherent set of four books for the final four years of primary school, or (particularly in England and Wales with the different primary leaving age) it can be for three years at primary and the first year of secondary. Varied stimuli are used and a range of thinking skills developed. A variety of themes ensures children can debate a range of moral and ethical issues.

Readers requiring more information or interested in in-service training can visit:

www.aude-education.co.uk or make an enquiry through

enquiries@aude-education.co.uk

'Carpe Diem, quam minimum, credula postero'

'Seize the day, and trust tomorrow as little as you may.'

Most of us do not know how to live in the present, yet many of the great philosophers have urged us to do so over the millennia. It is a vital point in the quest to know the Truth and learn about wisdom, and one that is directly linked to the raising of consciousness and our ability to know. The focusing exercise in this series of books seeks to give students some insight into the practice of this, and the first glimpses of a new world to explore.

. . . ' Til suddenly, and overwhence,
I looked upon your innocence.
For lifted clear and still strange
From the dark woven flow of change
Under a vast and starless sky
I saw the immortal moment lie.
One instant I, an instant, knew
As God knows all. And it and you
I, above time, oh, blind! Could see
In witless immortality . . .

Rupert Brooke
From 'The Dining-room Tea'

Sapere Aude - 'Dare to know'

CONTENTS

Why Philosophy with Children?

When people are first introduced to the idea of philosophy with children they are often dismissive. What is the point of teaching children philosophy when the curriculum is already overcrowded, and to what purpose? They envisage lessons on existentialism, or the life and thoughts of Schopenhauer. The first point to make therefore, is that this is practical philosophy - it is about the process, not the teaching of facts. We are not interested in facts about Kant, Wittgenstein, or even Socrates, but we are interested in the process of exploring philosophical questions through Socratic questioning. It is the dialogue that is important!

Raising pupil attainment is something that is currently of high political profile, and consequently in a climate of constant testing and league tables, is never far from the consciousness of either individual teachers or school managers. Raising attainment has been described as requiring effective teaching, and tackling the barriers to learning. These will depend on at least four factors:

- The extent to which early years experiential deficits are analysed and addressed;
- The extent to which there is a focus on the processes of learning and teaching;
- The extent to which learning and teaching is harmonised with the way in which the brain works;
- **The extent to which children are supported and challenged to think for themselves.**

In terms of raising pupil attainment, these might be looked upon as something like the tiers of a wedding cake, with each level somewhat dependent on the others. Also, however, it should be realised that attainment can only be raised to a certain level with each strategy. Therefore for each child to reach full potential, the final level of developing improved thinking skills must be accessed, and this is where a 'philosophy with children' programme is of great benefit.

It was earlier stated that the crux of such a programme is dialogue (or dialectic to use the Socratic term). This is much more than mere conversation, and offers the exciting possibility that one's own ideas and perceptions may change in the process. To use the jargon, this process begins to develop a 'community of enquiry', wherein teacher and pupils learn and develop together. Following the introduction of a stimulus such as a story or poem, philosophical questions are formulated from which the dialogue is derived. The key to developing good dialogue is the skill of the 'facilitator' in asking good, open-ended questions and encouraging the children to develop the same. These will include such questions as:-

- Can you say more about that?
- What makes you say that?
- Do you have any evidence for that view?
- How do you know that?
- Why? Why? Why?
- Is it possible to know if that is true?
- Does anyone else support that view?
- If...then what do you think about...? and so on.

1

It is through this process of dialogue that many things begin to take place:-
Thinking skills are developed. These include:

1. **Information Handling** - processing skills about analysing, interpreting, locating.
2. **Enquiry** - posing and defining problems, planning, predicting, testing conclusions.
3. **Reasoning** - giving reasons for opinions, making deductions, making judgements informed by evidence.
4. **Creative Thinking** - generating ideas, being imaginative in thinking, being innovative.
5. **Evaluation** - evaluating what is read or heard, developing criteria for judging.

In the next ten to fifteen years, one of the effects of globalisation will be that economies will become more and more knowledge based. If we don't have young people who can think well, the effect will be felt across the whole country, besides which those young people will not have been allowed to reach their full potential. It is vital that our education system begins to not only *allow* children to think, but *teaches* them to think. We spend so much effort teaching children the content of the subjects but don't actually teach them how to think, how to learn. If we don't change that, it will have tragic consequences. So, we must give children *time to think*, we must *teach them to think*, and we must *challenge them to think!* Philosophy plays a big part in this.

Life, of course, is not only about the economic well-being of the individual or the community, and this brings us to the second great strength of a 'philosophy with children' programme - it develops and strengthens the emotional intelligence. Daniel Goleman ('Emotional Intelligence', 'Working with Emotional Intelligence') quotes studies that show that a youngster's life chances are at least as much affected by emotional intelligence (EQ), as they are by IQ.
These intelligences include:

1. **Self-Awareness** - knowing how/what you are feeling and how it impinges on your work, having a realistic awareness of one's abilities.
2. **Self-Regulation** - handling emotions so they facilitate the task in hand, being conscientious.
3. **Motivation** - knowing what motivates us, persevering in the face of set-backs, striving to improve.
4. **Empathy** - sensing what other people are feeling, using that information in our dealings with them, being able to have a rapport with a wide range of people.
5. **Social Skills** - reading social situations, using skills to persuade, lead, negotiate.

As parents, as a society, we are not only concerned about how smart our children are, but *what kind of people* they grow up to be. When children explore moral and ethical questions, thoughts, behaviours - there opens up the possibility of even seeing the causes for these. This is a very empowering process because it brings the youngster to a point where *choice* is possible instead of habitual behaviour. This is *real* learning. It begins to have an effect on the whole community, whether that community is a family, a class, a school, or indeed society itself. For example, how do we get a just society? Imposing rules (laws) from the outside doesn't seem to work too well! It is better when the regulation comes from the 'inside', with each citizen being self-regulated through having the self-knowledge to make informed choices! Teaching about citizenship is also politically high profile at the moment - how much better when it is not just another set of facts, but part of a process of discovering what it is like to be a citizen! Philosophy can play a powerful role in this.

The third main strength of the philosophy programme is that it develops spiritual intelligence (SQ). This includes:

1. Having vision and values.
2. Seeing holistically - that is seeing the unity of things around us.
3. Being 'field independent' - being able to work against convention.
4. Spontaneously adaptive - being able to learn as situations are developing and use that information to affect the situation.

This aspect is seen as being further along the spectrum from emotional intelligence. It is about knowledge of myself, not as a collection of attributes, but in essence. Not myself, but my Self - that which I am.

As Chief Seattle, a Suquamish chief, said in 1854, 'The earth does not belong to man, man belongs to the earth. All things are connected like the blood that connects us all. Man did not weave the web of life, he is merely a strand in it. Whatever he does to the web, he does to himself'. Hopefully we can all move towards being as spiritually intelligent as he was!

As very young children begin to explore the world around them they touch, smell, and even taste everything and anything they can get their hands on. As they move into the world of language they begin to ask questions about everything - why, why, why. There is a natural spirit of enquiry that seeks to know 'What is this creation and what is my relationship to it?' Little philosophers abound! Unfortunately, in most cases this natural curiosity is largely knocked out of them by being ignored or told not to ask silly questions! The philosophy programme with children seeks to restore what is in fact absolutely natural, and build on this as cognitive development allows - then a 'community of enquiry' is born! In this, children learn about the process of learning and also about themselves as learners.

Besides pupil development, the process helps create powerful professionals who can naturally transfer the method to other curricular areas. Again, it is about the process of learning, not about imparting information.

In Clackmannanshire (Central Scotland), an initiative is underway to introduce this philosophy programme to eight to eleven year olds in every primary school in the Authority. It is built on research from around the world, showing that quality dialogue within a community of enquiry approach is a powerful developer of cognitive and emotional abilities. A new, detailed study is underway to monitor and assess the specific effectiveness of the programme, but already the anecdotal evidence is excellent. This programme is also being introduced by Nottinghamshire Council. A 'philosophy with children' programme strengthens and develops cognitive abilities and emotional literacy. It is a very powerful vehicle which empowers youngsters to become better learners and 'better', more fulfilled people. Use of the 'community of enquiry' method also greatly develops teachers as powerful professionals.

A Community of Enquiry

Developing the 'Socratic Method' within the Classroom

A community of enquiry is a group engaged in exploring ideas through dialogue. Dialogue using the 'Socratic method' is using open-ended questioning (described in detail in the section on 'Skilful Questioning') to explore issues and enquire after Truth. It is different to conversation, which is often just a stating of personal views without justification or reason. Stating positions on an issue and simply being tolerant of the positions of others does not lead anywhere, whereas a dialogue is an active process in which the participants can aid each others understanding. There is the possibility, and even the expectation, that one's views will change and develop through dialogue. The process of dialogue also facilitates a deeper engagement between all participants *(including the teacher)* and between the participants and what is under discussion. This greatly enhances learning. Professor Matthew Lipman describes the process as being similar to a sailing boat tacking against the wind - it has to go backwards and forwards across the wind but it also makes progress in a forward direction.

A community of enquiry has a rational structure and a moral structure. The former is about how to go about exploring ideas through dialogue and is detailed in the criteria of part 'B' of the evaluation form at the end of this section. It includes such aspects as ensuring that participants:

- Ask open and inviting questions
- Give evidence and examples
- Make comparisons
- Summarise and evaluate
- Seek clarification

The moral structure includes the application of emotional intelligence and could be called the 'spirit of enquiry'. It also includes the rules of behaviour necessary for a group activity such as one person being allowed to speak at a time. Further detail in part 'A' of the evaluation form includes ensuring that pupils:

- Focus attention on the speaker
- Don't 'put down' others
- Are not forced to speak
- Respect others' views
- Are truthful
- Are open minded

Pupils should sit in a position in which they can see each other, and this very much depends on the layout of the classroom. Some people use a circle, but with a whole class this can mean large distances between people (i.e. from one side of the circle to the other) and this is not helpful in developing a supportive, inclusive atmosphere. A horseshoe, semi-circular shape is often useful.

The teacher's role is often called 'facilitator' in the current jargon, and this is to show that it is not a traditional one of imparting knowledge or facts, but one of helping the process of the dialogue. This is done through being an active participant and at the same time stimulating the process by:

- Focusing attention on important points.
- Modelling good questioning, for example, by asking for clarification, reasons, evidence etc.
- Encouraging pupils in appropriate behaviours, such as how to respond to each other, to listen to each other, and so on.
- Rewarding positive contributions with praise.
- Not being content with conversation.
- **Directing the discussion towards Truth.** *

The teacher's role is a dynamic one - sometimes being an ordinary participant, sometimes guiding a pupil to deeper involvement, sometimes ensuring that the agreed rules are adhered to. It takes practice!

It is important to note that the community of enquiry approach is just as relevant to other curricular areas as it is to the 'philosophy with children' programme. It is a powerful tool in learning and teaching. Dylan William and Paul Black (King's College London) have expounded a similar approach to formative assessment in their book 'Inside the Black Box'.

* ". . . the process of philosophical enquiry is guided by the ideal of truth (where possible) and, in practical matters, by the ideal of good judgement or reasonableness."
Roger Sutcliffe - Chair of SAPERE

The Structure of Each Philosophy Session

In this section the structure of each philosophy session is described, and the details of each element.

THE FOCUSING EXERCISE. This is a simple but extremely powerful exercise that helps people focus their attention and be 'in the present'. Its simplicity is its strength and also its weakness. It is easy to do, but also easy for children to think they are doing it when in fact they are not.

The exercise consists of simply 'giving' attention out through the senses for two or three minutes. This creates a highly alert yet peaceful condition. For the short time (literally two minutes) that it takes to do it, in value for time it is probably the most powerful aspect of the programme! The first purpose is that of calming - a physiological harmonisation takes place in which breathing and heart rate slow and there should be mental and emotional calmness. This is a good state in which to be able to think! Secondly, there is the notion of 'giving' attention. Instead of our levels of wakefulness (consciousness) being largely haphazard and habit driven, the individual begins to have a choice, and to exhibit control over this. This is very powerful in relation to raising attainment and exhibiting emotional intelligence. This very important technique of learning to 'be in the present' or 'be here now' was reported in a well-researched article entitled 'Mindfulness' in the British Medical Journal of November 2001.

To do 'the exercise', ask children to sit in an upright position with straight back and feet flat on the floor. Initially, explain the reasons for doing the exercise. Tell them that they can use it whenever they choose - before a test, doing a piece of writing, when they feel angry or upset, and so on. Be sure to include before a football game! For athletes to be 'in the zone', that area of peak performance, they must be in the present and fully focused. Children should listen to the sound of the teacher's voice as the instructions are read out and should try to follow, focusing only on what they themselves are doing and not on anyone else.

"First give your attention to the sense of touch. Feel the weight of your feet on the floor ... Your body on the chair ... Your clothes on the skin ... Pause. Now, using sight, and without naming things in the mind, see colours ... shapes ... the space between the shapes. Pause. Now using the sense of hearing, hear any sounds close at hand *(e.g. within the classroom)* ... now let the hearing gradually run right out until the furthest sounds can be heard ... Pause. Now try to hold that awareness for a few moments."

It is important that children do not just sit there daydreaming - this is a conscious activity. A short period of questioning children on the experience can be useful sometimes, but remember it is not about hearing a bus, a bird and so on, but rather developing a growing awareness of where their attention was - was it on the looking and listening or on thinking about what they were going to do after school?

Sometimes in the Teaching Notes attention is drawn to particular aspects of the exercise. This is to provide variety and also to deepen awareness of the technique. Many teachers find it useful to practise the exercise daily and at times when the class needs to settle or focus attention.

LINKING WITH THE PREVIOUS WEEK

This is simply good practice and reinforces in the mind what has taken place the week before, thereby strengthening memory. It also provides an opportunity for children to bring forward new evidence and experience from during the week. Thinking is not something that only takes place on Wednesdays from ten until eleven!

PAIR/GROUP WORK

This provides an opportunity to check that children have understood the literal meaning of the story or poem, and more importantly, is where there is a planned focus on one or more of the thinking skills. These are built into the programme. Also important about this stage is that it is very 'inclusive'. Children who may not initially speak in a whole class forum can gain confidence that their ideas are important and accepted in a small-scale setting.

THE STIMULUS

The story or poem is read aloud by the teacher.

DIALOGUE

The *key* to the whole programme. This is the Socratic method of questioning or 'dialectic'. Prof. Matthew Lipman says this is not 'mere' conversation, but 'an inquiry, an exploration of ideas - a quest. It follows a line of investigation like a detective'. The 'Questions for Thinking' are used to stimulate this process, but it is important to note that these are not to be slavishly followed through to the end if the dialogue is flowing. The section on 'Questioning' in these notes will help build the skill of being a good facilitator of a dialogue. It is not to present yourself as the expert in philosophy (and it is assumed that you are not), or yet to move the group to think as you think. It is to coordinate and enhance the dialogue by modelling open questioning, by encouraging all to take part, by not being content always with first answers and knowing how to allow the child to think more deeply by further questioning. Look at the criteria in the 'Assessment of a Philosophy Session' for further examples.

Dialogue is important because it stimulates a deeper engagement between pupils and teacher and can take learning to a deeper level of understanding. It requires the teacher to move from being a dispenser of information to a facilitator of learning - the method can be used to great effect across the curriculum. Dialogue stimulates thinking and emotional intelligence, bringing with it self-confidence.

CLOSURES

These are brief ways of closing the dialogue and in essence, provide a variety of ways of drawing the attention of the children to how their thinking has progressed during the session.

THOUGHT FOR THE WEEK

Each week a practical idea drawn from the theme of the story or poem is highlighted to provide some 'homework'. In the main it is looking for evidence in real situations of an aspect of the theme. This should be encouraged but entirely natural and unforced! Nothing will put children off more quickly. It is useful if the 'Thought for the Week' is displayed on the classroom wall for reference and as a reminder.

The Importance of Skilful Questioning

Good dialogue is dependent on skilful questioning, both by the teacher as facilitator and by pupils as participants. It is at the heart of a 'community of enquiry'.

Research has repeatedly shown that in the main, skilful questioning does not take place in most classrooms. Edwards and Westgate (1987) showed that before attending school, children generate more than 50% of questions. These same children asked less than 5% of questions in their nursery schools! In secondary school, students were still asking less than 15% of the questions. There is no reason to think that things have changed much since these studies. The above figures are about quantity and not quality, but studies looking at the nature of questioning in classrooms also show there is room for great improvement. A typical pattern (Purkey 1978, Dillon 1983, Morgan and Saxton 1994) is where the teacher asks many closed, low-level questions, often requiring only one word answers. If an answer is not forthcoming from the child that is asked, the teacher immediately moves to someone else or provides the answer. A small percentage of the class answer the vast majority of the questions. However, by learning simple strategies and using a wide variety of open questions, skilful questioning can be developed.

A. CREATING GOOD DIALOGUE THROUGH QUESTIONING.

Some kinds of questions are _not_ very useful in developing good dialogue and a 'community of enquiry'.

These include:

Closed Questions - these often require one word, factual answers. 'Have you read this book about Aztecs?' 'Where did you get that information?'

Multiple Questions - these can be too complex for children to process all parts so that usually only the first part is answered. 'Tell me what you think of that, and whether or not you think it is reasonable, then compare it with what we said earlier about . . . '

Leading Questions - these are often used to influence the students (although sometimes unconsciously), and so can lead to a closing down of thinking and ideas, rather than an expansion.

By using a wide variety of questions, different kinds of thinking can be stimulated, such as reasoning, creative, analytical, and evaluative.

Such questions can include:

CLARIFYING
    What reasons do you have for saying that?
    What do you mean by that?
    Can you explain more about that?
    Have you an example of that?
    What makes you so sure of that?

8

PROBING THE SUPERFICIAL

Why do you think that?

What is the cause of that?

What makes you say that?

Why . . . Why . . . Why?

EXPLORING ALTERNATIVE VIEWS

Is there another point of view?

Can you put it another way?

Are you and s/he contradicting each other?

What is the difference between your view and . . . . . ?

SCAFFOLDING

What do you think about . . . . . . ?

What is the reason for . . . . . . ?

If . . . . . . then what do you think about . . . . . . ?

You said . . . . . . but what about . . . . . . ?

SEEKING EVIDENCE

How do you know that?

What makes you say that?

What is your evidence?

What are your reasons?

What makes you so sure?

TESTING IMPLICATIONS

Is that consistent with what you first said?

What would be the consequences of . . . . . . ?

How do we know if that is true?

How can we test that in practice?

EVALUATING.

Who can summarise the main points for us?

Can anyone say where our thinking has taken us?

What new ideas have we developed?

If . . . . . . why . . . . . . ?

Of course it is not possible to hold all these questions in mind at once, and certainly not useful to have a list in front of you during an enquiry - that would certainly stultify the dialogue. However, through awareness of a range of questions, one's repertoire can be gradually increased in practice.

9

B. STRATEGIES FOR GOOD QUESTIONING.

- **GIVE THINKING TIME**
  This is absolutely critical. One study showed that with increased thinking time:
  pupils gave longer answers;
  more pupils volunteered answers;
  more pupils asked questions, and
  answers given were more analytical, evaluative and creative.

- **SECOND-QUESTIONING**
  Send the ball back! This is the skill of knowing when to repeatedly question someone on each answer - but with care and finesse. This forces the person to think more deeply.

- **ASK _ALL_ PUPILS**
  This improves thinking, attainment and discipline. Consciously make sure that over a period of time all pupils are involved, but avoid pressuring children to answer. Encourage contributions through praise.

- **PROVIDE CUES AND ASSISTANCE**
  If a child is struggling to answer a question, provide cues and assistance (scaffold) rather than just moving straight on to another pupil.

- **SLOW THE RATE OF QUESTIONING**
  Quality is better than quantity!

- **LISTEN**
  A skilful questioner is a good listener. Good listening allows the listener to be informed, and so makes their next question more intelligent. This point is related to the one above.

- **WITHHOLD JUDGEMENT**
  As children give responses and answer questions, respond in a non-judgemental way by thanking children for their contributions, and continuing to take further responses. Encourage alternative views.

- **KEEP IT SIMPLE**
  Use simple but appropriate language.

Thinking Maps

'Thinking maps' are also known as model maps, webbing maps, learning maps, and various other names including at least one that is registered copyright!

Thinking maps are just that - a guide to our thinking on something, whether as a study guide to remember a piece of work (book, concept, area of study, etc.), or as a method of showing development of an idea or even helping in the actual process of developing it. Thinking maps help us remember - and remembering means just that, remembering. That is, putting back the 'members' (parts) or making a unified whole out of the diversity of the different ideas. This implies also a 'making sense of'. A thinking map is a visual organisation of ideas that shows both the overall view and the detail.

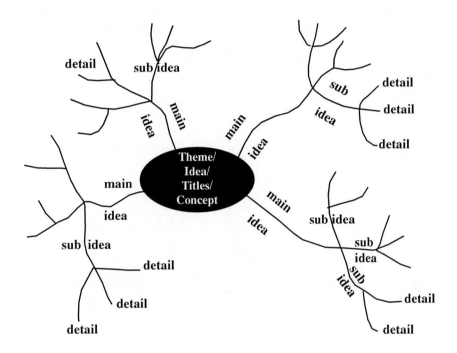

A thinking map not only brings clarity to the central idea, but fits itself to the individual's thought patterns as it is constructed. They may be used for reviewing work previously studied, finding out what is known about something, and as a tool to explain something to others. They are also useful in developing lines of thought or concepts.

To introduce thinking maps it is best to first talk through the concept with pupils, then show them one fully constructed, such as the one given above. Next, collaboratively build one on the board so that children see the various steps in construction. Use a theme or topic recently studied or well known to the pupils.

When constructing a thinking map:

- Begin by writing the theme, title, or main ideas in the centre of the page.
- Put in the first radiating arms by writing in the main ideas that come to mind.
- Develop these, one at a time, by writing in the sub-ideas, then the detail.
- If other major ideas occur, write them in and develop them.
- Some people like to use colour (e.g. a different colour for each idea) or draw little pictures. Each individual should decide whether this is important to them, and use the devices if they help.

For the map to be of use, once it is constructed it must be actively and consciously used using language to 'tell the story' of what it shows. That is, instead of a cursory glance, each branch must be described right out through the main ideas to the sub-ideas and the detail. This can be done silently 'in the mind' or out loud. Each repetition of this process reinforces what the map contains.

Thinking Through Mysteries

The use of 'mysteries' to develop thinking skills was initially developed by Dr David Leat and the Thinking Skills Research Group at Newcastle University. Originally it was within the context of geography in the secondary school, but it is a particularly powerful strategy for developing a wide range of thinking skills and can be successfully used across a range of areas. I am indebted to David Leat for his openness and support in sharing materials, and in particular the basis of the accompanying table regarding diagnostic and formative assessment.

In this book a mystery is an activity where a short story is used to set up a scenario in which an event (usually involving an ethical or moral dilemma) takes place. The pupils then have to use evidence, provided on numerous separate slips of paper, to explore possible solutions.

A wide range of thinking skills are involved in the process of trying to find a solution, including:

- Information processing skills
- Enquiry skills
- Reasoning skills
- Creative Thinking Skills
- Evaluation Skills

The development of thinking is further enhanced by the teacher being able to help a group or individual by 'scaffolding'. That is, by skilful intervention at critical points to enable the group to continue to move forward in their exploration, when otherwise they may have come to a complete halt.

This is related to the Vygotsky's concept of a Zone of Proximal Development (ZPD). This is the gap between what a child can achieve alone, and what they can achieve with adult guidance. Through being challenged and guided to enter this zone, the baseline of what can be achieved unaided is raised.

Not only is thinking developed through this strategy, but it also provides an insight into the child's thinking, and so can be used as a diagnostic tool. What the teacher can observe about the physical organisation and manipulation of the evidence (slips of paper) is a reflection of the thinking processes and their sophistication. Dialogue, which is the key to this programme as a whole is also a strong feature in the 'mysteries' elements.

The Thinking Skills Research Group identified five possible stages which may be observed when students are engaged in a mystery.

THE DISPLAY STAGE
At this stage groups familiarise themselves with the information. Some groups distribute the slips like cards then take turns in reading them out. Others just spread them out and begin to sift through them. The purpose here is to begin to come to terms with the information although not all groups achieve this successfully unaided.

THE SETTING STAGE

Data begins to be organised into sets. Generally, common elements provide the links. These may include items involving members of the same family, people present at a particular incident, or more sophisticated sets such as 'stronger evidence' and 'red herrings'.

Even at this stage the strategy may indicate cognitive ability, for example low achievers may form sets on the basis of common vocabulary such as the names of characters or places. Higher achieving groups may form sets with broader themes such as 'anyone who was at the scene of the incident'. Lower achievers may have a pile of information slips spread randomly over the table, whilst those with a better approach build up sets in columns or blocks. A further refinement is the creation of sub-sets, although most groups form a reject pile.

THE SEQUENCING AND WEBBING STAGE

Some groups may not get beyond the setting stage but most groups begin to form relationships between sets or between single pieces of evidence. This may be in terms of a line of development (sequencing) or in multi-linear relationships (webbing) creating a web. Inference is commonly needed to build these relationships.

THE REWORKING STAGE

Reworking can be simply moving one piece of evidence from one set to another, or can involve wholesale reorganisation and reworking of sets. It may be the re-examination of the reject pile looking for items of significance. Many groups do not re-work their sets, but it seems to be a characteristic of high performance groups that they have no hesitation in breaking up sets and looking for new connections.

THE ABSTRACT STAGE

A few groups are able to leave the physical data and continue to discuss possible solutions having internalised enough of the data. This is a high level of working.

Using Mysteries for Diagnostic and Formative Assessment

Stage	Observation	Possible Meaning Diagnostic Assessment	Possible Action Formative Assessment
Display	Pupils cannot start.	Inability to read data items. Inability to comprehend. Inability to find a starting strategy.	Talk to Special Needs / Learning Support. Simplify text. Ask pupils: "What do you think this means?" Ask "How could you go about starting to sort the information?"
Setting	Inability to group data items.	Inability to identify characteristics that would inform classification. Inability to identify items of greater importance. Inability to draw upon prior knowledge.	Identify a characteristic of a data item and ask "Can you find me another that is to do with X?" Ask "What would make this an important piece of information?" Refresh memory of past experiences or learning.
Sequencing and Webbing	Setted data unsorted. Line of data items. Isolated groups.	Inability to identify sequence of events or causal relationship. Causation seen as a simple linear sequence or causal chain. Unable to make links between factors/groups.	Ask "Do you think this happened before or after that?" "Why?" Consult reject pile for key data. "Do you think this piece might help?" Invite pupils to connect a data item to a point along the linear sequence. Ask "Is there any link between this group and that one?"
Reworking	No reworking. Reject pile ignored. Bizarre theories.	Reluctance to reconsider alternatives. Ditto. Lack of critical evaluation.	Question logic or invite them to compare with another group of items. Bring items from reject pile to their attention. Ask questions such as, "So you are arguing...?" "How likely is it that...?" Challenge **them** to justify ignoring **particular** data.
Abstract	No reference back to data.	Over generalisation or lack of critical evaluation.	Check their understanding of the conceptual themes. Refer pupils back to data to check theory.

Critical Challenges

Critical Challenges are activities that have been devised to develop a range of thinking skills, and in particular, critical thinking. There is nothing new about the actual skills involved in thinking, although their names may have changed over time - from Bloom's taxonomy to the list described by Fisher and others.

1. The activities in this part of the programme aim to develop information handling, enquiry skills, reasoning, creative thinking and evaluation. Critical thinking brings together different elements of the above and involves developing in children the ability to make reasoned judgements about particular situations or in particular contexts. This, therefore, is about the process of analysing, problem solving and decision-making. However, it is not just this process, but rather the process set within certain criteria that begin to define the nature of critical thinking.

2. Bailin includes as examples of criteria for judging good critical thinking, such things as accuracy, coherence, clarity, feasibility, fairness and plausibility. These would be considered in relation to the process described above, of analysing information, solving problems and making decisions. It is also important that attitudes of mind conducive to critical thinking be fostered. These include such things as having an open-mind, being fair-minded and having a critical enquiring attitude.

The Critical Challenges have certain important elements built into them. Firstly, they are strongly rooted in **dialogue**, as is being developed through the 'community of enquiry' approach in the philosophy sessions. Secondly, **group working** is an important feature, both to develop confidence in the dialogical skills and to encourage the inclusion of those who are initially reticent to take part. Thirdly, reporting back from small group to class forum and justifying positions through reasoned argument, clarifies thinking through the process of articulating one's thoughts **aloud**. This is a very powerful mechanism. Finally, the activities develop the skills involved in the process of critical thinking, as described earlier.

The Critical Challenges in the book take three slightly different forms as they seek to encompass the range of skills involved. There are two examples of each type, which lead to the final form in Book 3 and so on to Mysteries. The Teaching Notes for each of the challenges is particularly full in order to make clear the tasks involved in each particular challenge.

During each classroom session the children have a short story or article to 'set the scene', then have some related pieces of information to analyse. Decision-making and problem-solving activities flow from this initial analysis. The pieces of information are on small pieces of card with one item per card, and the children work in groups completing specified tasks.

As the children work with the information cards, the teacher moves between groups listening to what is being said, and observing what is being done with the information. The accompanying grid will assist in gaining an impression of the competence of each group or even individual. The various criteria can be highlighted to the children during the report back sessions by praising contributions of high level (expert) examples of the criteria. This will lead to their further development.

1.   Fisher, R. 'Teaching Thinking'
2.   Bailin, S. 'What is Critical about Critical Thinking?'

Critical Thinking

This matrix may be used in two ways, and with either the Critical Challenges or the Mysteries (Books 3 & 4). It should be used when observing and listening to a group analysing and organising the information supplied for the activities.

- The first is in gaining a broad impression of the quality of critical thinking in a group or class. To do this, read and become familiar with the criteria in general terms. In listening to the group (class) notice when various criterion are exhibited, and by seeing whether the bulk of comments heard are related to columns one, two or three, an impression of the general quality of the critical thinking can be gained. It is easier to do with the matrix at hand to refer to.

- The second, more sophisticated method, gains a more accurate picture of the quality of the thinking, and also can be related to formative assessment.

1. Firstly, copy the blank matrix on to an acetate.

2. Place the acetate over the full version of the matrix. Then, using an acetate felt pen, put a tally mark in the appropriate box when an example of one of the criteria in that box is heard. (It is best to just assess a group and not a class at any one time).

3. At the end of the session, get a score by giving 5 points for every mark in column three, 3 points for marks in column two, and 1 for marks in column one.

4. Use the information formatively by discussing with the group where the bulk of the marks fell, and what this means in terms of specific criterion.
   Explain and discuss fully, so pupils are aware of what constitutes good critical thinking. Use examples from their own comments, and let them recall examples. In this way, the children will seek to improve in the next dialogue, and deliberately employ better thinking.

5. If the groups had the same constituents, two results several months apart could be compared.

CRITERION REFERENCED MATRIX FOR CRITICAL THINKING	NOT SKILLED	COMPETENT	EXPERT
CLARITY	No clarifying questions. Arguments not clear. Muddled ideas. Does not define ideas or arguments.	Asks for some clarification. Tries to be clear in expressing ideas. Sometimes follows a line of argument.	Asks clarifying questions. Clear ideas expressed. Follows a line of argument. Defines things clearly. Clarifies meaning aloud.
COHERENCE	No linking ideas. Has diverse ideas. Decisions made on 'whims' not based on information. Cannot summarise group dialogue.	Can take 2 or 3 ideas or pieces of information and integrate them. Beginning to be able to summarise.	Puts several ideas together. Unifies. Intergrates pieces of information to make a decision. Can summarise well. Exhibits a structure to an argument.
ACCURACY	Not aware of contexts. Cannot identify irrelevance. Evidence and arguments are unclear and imprecise.	Makes effort to define. Is aware of irrelevance and usually ignores it. Makes effort to be precise.	Defines terms appropriate to the context. Can identify and ignore irrelevance. Tries to give precise information and descriptions.
FAIRNESS	Is biased. Works only from habitual ideas. Not interested in other's views. Ignores or is not aware of a broad range of issues.	Is aware of concept of open-mindedness. Tries to be open-minded and examine issues. Makes efforts to consider others' views and take account of their feelings.	Is open minded. Examines all issues. Is open to alternative views. Considers other peoples views. Exhibits emotional intelligence (takes account of others' feelings and understanding).
ORIGINALITY	Doesn't show originality. Reticent to try new ideas / methods. Doesn't seek alternative solutions.	Sometimes intentionally seeks alternatives. Sometimes shows original ideas. Beginning to open up to new	Seeks alternative solutions/ conclusions. Offers original ideas and arguments. Has a willingness to try new methods.
STRATEGIES	No organisational strategies shown. Doesn't show problem solving strategies. Cannot begin to organise.	Exhibits some organisational strategies. Beginning to draw sequences from data. Problem solving ideas are discussed and tested.	Uses various strategies to organise information. Follows problem-solving steps. Exhibits logical patterns of analysing information on cards. Can work in the abstract.
CRITICAL QUESTIONING / ATTITUDE	Accepts "first answers and explanations." Accepts assumptions. Has a narrow perspective. Does not probe for depth.	Is aware of the importances of reasons and evidence. Beginning to question options and assumptions. Showing more awareness of alternative views.	Seeks evidence. Probes explanations. Questions assumptions. Looks for alternative views. Shows an eagerness to enquire further.

19

Assessment and Evaluation

As this section is being written, Tiger Woods has just come off the course after playing a round in the British Open. Asked if he would now be going for a well-earned beer, he replied that he would be going to the practice area to 'hit some balls for an hour'. Even when you are the best in the world at something, there is still room for improvement - and this same attitude is a good one to adopt in relation to facilitating philosophy with children. Indeed, in a true 'community of enquiry' in which the group (which includes the teacher) develops as a unit, adopting an attitude of limitless possibilities is rather useful. With that in mind, three proformas are offered to assist with the development of the method.

OBSERVATION SHEET:
This may be used either by a teacher reflecting on a philosophy session which has recently taken place, or more usefully, by a teacher who is using the programme observing someone else facilitating a session. Working with a partner in this work can be very useful. If the latter strategy is employed, subsequent discussion of the comments is an important part of the process - more dialogue!

ASSESSING DIALOGUE:
Use of this sheet can help show the progress made in effecting good dialogue. The sheet must be completed by a person other than the facilitator, but one who also is familiar with the programme. It is not envisaged that this be used very often, perhaps at the beginning and end of a year, especially if the group is just starting the programme. Making pupils familiar with the criteria over the course of a year is helpful in letting them develop the concept of what constitutes good dialogue. If working alone, video record ten minutes of the dialogue part of a session then analyse later in the same manner.

EVALUATION FORM:
This comprehensive sheet covers both the rational structure for exploring ideas through dialogue, (the 'technical' aspects of what constitutes good dialogue), and also the moral structure which includes those aspects of emotional intelligence which by their nature allow good dialogue to take place. For example the former includes such things as supporting ones assertions with evidence and asking open-ended questions, whilst the latter includes respecting the ideas of others and using positive body language to encourage others.

This sheet can be used in several ways. It can be used in similar fashion to the last two, by teachers reflecting on the work of their own groups and by a teacher observing a colleague. Very usefully this sheet can be used with pupils, allowing them to reflect on, and evaluate, their own work. It is important to spend time with pupils looking at each point and discussing what it means in practice. This focus on the criteria again is very useful in helping children to understand what is considered 'good dialogue' and why.

Philosophy With Children
Observation Sheet

In observing a philosophy session, jot down strengths, weaknesses and points for discussion. Remember to note - *good comments by children; evidence or reasons given by children, linking of several ideas by an individual or several people, range of questions by children, has the group 'moved forward' through dialogue?*

The Calming Exercise:

The Stimulus:

Individual/Pair/Group Work:

The Enquiry Through Dialogue:

General Comments:

Assessing Classroom Dialogue

Class: **Date:**

Duration:

Behaviour	Tally Marks	Total
Pupil 1. Occurrence of pupils asking a question.		
2. Occurrence of pupil supporting their view / opinion with a reason.		
3. Occurrence of a pupil agreeing or disagreeing with the view of another pupil, and giving a reason.		
4. Occurrence of pupil offering a reviewing or evaluating comment. (See ideas under 'Skilful Questioning' section).		
5. Occurrence of pupil directly addressing another pupil.		
Teacher 6. Occurrence of teacher asking a question requiring a one word or factual response. *(Not useful for dialogue).*		
7. Occurrence of teacher asking an open-ended question. (This includes follow-up questions).		

Developed, with permission, from work by S. Trickey

Evaluation Form For Philosophical Enquiry

A. THE ETHOS OR SPIRIT OF ENQUIRY

(Listening and Responding)

SCALE:

0 = hardly ever, **1** = some, sometimes **2** = most, most of the time **3** = almost all the time

1. Did people focus their attention on the speaker? (Attentiveness)	0	1	2	3
2. Did people avoid interrupting or rushing the speaker? (Patience)	0	1	2	3
3. Did people encourage each other to speak? (Altruism) (e.g. by smiling, taking turns, etc.)	0	1	2	3
4. Did people respond to the previous speaker? (Responsiveness)	0	1	2	3
5. Did people respond to the main questions being asked? (Tenacity)	0	1	2	3
6. Did people keep their speeches brief and to the point? (Relevance)	0	1	2	3
7. Did people recall others' ideas and put their names to them? (respect)	0	1	2	3
8. Did people try to build on others' ideas? (Constructiveness)	0	1	2	3
9. Did people listen to ideas different from their own? (Tolerance)	0	1	2	3
10. Did people show a willingness to change their minds? (Openess)	0	1	2	3

B. THINKING TOGETHER

(Questioning and Reasoning)

SCALE:

0 = not observed, **1** = observed at least once **2** = observed now and then **3** = observed often

11. Did people ask open and inviting questions?	0	1	2	3
12. Did people ask for clarifications of meaning?	0	1	2	3
13. Did people question assumptions of fact or value?	0	1	2	3
14. Did people ask for examples or evidence?	0	1	2	3
15. Did people ask for reasons or criteria?	0	1	2	3
16. Did people give examples or counter-examples?	0	1	2	3
17. Did people give reasons or justifications?	0	1	2	3
18. Did people offer or explore alternative viewpoints?	0	1	2	3
19. Did people make comparisons or analogies?	0	1	2	3
20. Did people make distinctions?	0	1	2	3

BLOCK ONE

In this block, the following thinking skills have a particular focus in the pair/group work.

Sequencing	=	Session 1, 3, 9
Classification	=	Session 5
Analysing	=	Session 7

Block 1 • Session 1

'Mum's Helper' Teaching Notes

1. Remind children that they can look outwards and inwards. That is, through using the senses (outwards) and by knowing or 'watching' our thoughts (inwards). Both of these can happen whilst doing the exercise. Practise the exercise together.

2. Remind pupils that each week they will be asked to think about the last philosophy session, and bring forward any new evidence thoughts or ideas connected with it. They should know that philosophy and thinking do not just take place during the 1 hour lesson per week - good thinking can take place at anytime.

3. Read the story 'Mum's Helper'.

4. Ask children to remember three things that happened in the story, in the correct order, and then share these with a partner.

5. Working in groups of 3 or 4, get children to discuss what they thought was the theme or 'inner meaning' of the story.

6. Move to the 'Questions for Thinking' to stimulate the dialogue.

7. For a closure activity, get children to think of one idea mentioned today that is important to them.

8. Discuss the 'Thought for the Week'.

Sarah was having a hard time at home. Her Mum had broken her leg, and Sarah was finding it hard to play a much bigger role in the family. What would be the consequences for the family if she failed?

MUM'S HELPER

Sarah shut the front door and swung her school bag onto her back. It felt as though half the day had gone already, she had been up since half past six. She hadn't done her maths homework either but she knew Mrs Barker would let her off. Making allowances, it was called.

'Hi, Sarah!' It was her best friend, Helen. 'Are you coming round tonight? We can watch the tennis on Sky.'

Sarah shook her head. 'Got to do some shopping after school and help mum with the dinner.'

Helen looked at her with pity. 'Oh, yeah. I forgot. How is your mum?'

Sarah shrugged. 'OK.'

'Did she break her leg, or what?' asked Helen.

'She had an operation on it and can't put any weight on it for two months,' explained Sarah. 'And you can't do anything when you've got crutches and you're balancing on one leg.'

After school as Sarah walked round the supermarket she thought of Helen watching the tennis. They were both mad about tennis and loved to play but everything had changed since mum had her operation.

Gran had taken time off work to look after her and her brother Lee while their mum had been in hospital but now there was no-one to help. If only their mum and dad hadn't split up. But she'd wished that a thousand times.

'Hello, Mum!' she called, letting herself in the front door. Angus, their Westie, flew at her ankles, barking, and she bent down to stroke him.

There was the thudding of crutches from upstairs and her mum's face appeared at the top of the stairs.

'Hello, love. I was just having a rest but I'm coming down now.' She promptly sat down and began to shuffle downstairs on her bottom.

'I'll fetch your crutches, Mum.' Sarah smiled at the comical sight as her mum caught her eye. Then they both laughed. Angus barked again, joining in the fun.

'What an indignity,' said Mum. 'But it's safer.'

Sarah made the dinner while her mum sat in the kitchen and told her what to do. Later, Lee came home from a friend's house and they all sat and ate. Then Sarah got the washing out of the machine and loaded it into the dryer.

'Lee's in bed,' said her mum, hopping into the kitchen. 'I'm off too. I'm tired and my leg hurts. Try and do your homework, love, and be in bed by nine o'clock. Don't forget to feed Angus.'

Sarah kissed her mum goodnight and looked at her watch. It was already seven-thirty and she still had to do the washing up. It would be great to have a dishwasher like Helen's mum, but no chance of that.

That night as Sarah climbed into bed and set her alarm for six-thirty, she thought about how strange it was to be responsible for all these domestic problems as if she were an adult and to be the last one to go to bed. Things had certainly turned upside down.

She didn't have time to take Angus for a walk the next morning.

Sarah was late that morning and she had to run all the way to school. Lee had already gone with his friend earlier while she was helping her mum get dressed and make the beds. Now she ran panting into school just as the bell rang.

'Brought your racquet?' asked Helen.

Sarah clasped a hand on her mouth. How could she have forgotten? They were going to play at lunchtime and enter for the local under twelves tournament.

Helen was cross. 'I thought you loved tennis! We were going to be a doubles team, remember?' She turned her back on Sarah and banged her schoolbag onto her desk.

'I do love tennis,' said Sarah. 'But you know I have to help mum at the moment. There'll be time for tennis later, when she's better.'

'Huh,' said Helen. 'I don't see why you can't have some time off.'

Sarah did consider asking her mum if she could play in the tournament on Saturday. Maybe Gran could come over.

'Mum,' she began after dinner that evening. 'I wondered if . . .'

Her mum looked up at her and Sarah noticed that her eyes were tired and red-rimmed. Maybe she had been crying, she sometimes did when she felt very low.

'What, love?'

'I wondered if your leg was hurting?'

Her mum nodded. 'It is a bit, but it's not that. I really feel bad that you have to take on all this responsibility and work at your age. At ten you should be out with your friends, not doing housework. It's so frustrating, Sarah, not being able to do things. I could scream sometimes. If only things had worked out better . . .'

She means between her and Dad, thought Sarah.

'It's all right, Mum,' she said. And there went the tennis tournament. Well, she would still be under twelve next year. She could try then. She wished Helen could understand that when things cropped up in your life you couldn't just ignore them and hope that they would go away. They didn't. You had to get through them as best you could.

On Saturday morning Sarah was really tired and would have loved to lie in bed half the morning as she had done sometimes. She opened one eye and looked at her clock. Five past eight. She'd just have another ten minutes. Her mum usually did get her own breakfast so there was no real hurry.

Suddenly there was a crash and a yell from downstairs and Sarah leapt out of bed and ran down the stairs two at a time, her heart thudding. In the kitchen her mum lay on the floor, groaning.

'My leg,' she wailed. 'I tripped up over Angus and fell on my bad leg. It's agony. Phone Dr Harwood, love,' gasped her mother.

Within twenty minutes an ambulance arrived and the paramedics carefully lifted their mum onto the stretcher and took her out to the ambulance. Sarah and Lee went to the hospital as well.

During the morning their mum had an X-ray and the consultant told them that everything was all right. He asked if she had any help at home.

'Oh yes,' she'd said, putting an arm round each of her children. 'I have very good help.'

QUESTIONS FOR THINKING

1. In the story, Sarah had some things to do for her mum and some things she would have liked to do for herself - her own needs. What did Sarah think were her own needs?

2. Often we see to our own needs first. These are the things we want to do. What are some of these 'needs' for you?

3. Are these needs exactly the same for all of us? Where do they come from?

4. In the story, what were the family needs?

5. Why did Sarah choose to put the family needs first?

6. Why do people choose to do things for others even when it causes difficulties for themselves?

7. How did Sarah's feelings change at different times in the story? Why?

8. If what Sarah did was called 'Service', what do you think service is?

Thought for the Week

During the week, try to notice the times when you are doing something for someone else. Then try to see why you are doing it. What is the cause of the action?

Block 1 • Session 2

'Little Girl Be Careful' Teaching Notes

1. Remind the children again that when 'in the present' (moment) they are aware of both what is known through the senses and the fact that they are knowing or experiencing it. (For example, this is looking at something and at that moment knowing that you are seeing. It is making that conscious connection with what is under observation). Practise the exercise, trying to 'be in the present'.

2. Remember the story about 'Mum's Helper' and see what further ideas children can bring to last week's dialogue.

3. Read 'Little Girl Be Careful What You Say', getting the children to focus on the sound of your voice.

4. With a copy of the poem and working in pairs, get children to read it aloud to each other.

5. Get each person to quietly reflect on a possible theme for the poem, with reasons for their choice. Get children to share these with a partner, then each pair should join with another and again share the ideas. Each group should decide on the idea they think best describes the theme of the poem. When groups report back, build an ideas web on the board.

6. Move to the 'Questions for Thinking' to support the dialogue.

7. To conclude, ask pupils for the most important thing they have learned today about the power of words.

8. Discuss the 'Thought for the Week'.

Little Girl Be Careful What You Say

Little girl be careful what you say
when you make talk with words-
for words are made of syllables
and syllables, child, are made of air-
and air so thin - air is the breath of God-
air is finer than fire or mist,
finer than water or moonlight,
finer than spider-webs in the moon,
finer than water-flowers in the morning:
and words are strong, too,
stronger than potatoes, corn, fish, cattle,
and soft, too, soft as little pigeon eggs.
So, little girl, when you speak greetings,
when you tell jokes, make wishes or prayers,
be careful, be careful, be careful, be what you wish to be.

Carl Sandburg

QUESTIONS FOR THINKING

1. What did the poet say that words were made of?

2. What is the strong contrast that the poet makes in the poem?

3. In what way do you think words can be strong? What does the poet mean by this?

4. Why should the girl be careful in what she says?

5. Should we be careful in what we say? Why?

6. Are words real?

7. What does real mean?

8. Could words not be real?

9. The poet says '..be what you wish to be'. What does this mean?

10. Could words have power? How?

11. Do words make us be what we want to be? How?

Thought for the Week

During the week, try to be aware of the things that you say. Look for evidence as to whether words can be strong, and whether they have power. Do they govern your actions?

Block 1 • Session 3

'The Butterfly' Teaching Notes

1. Practise the exercise in focusing attention. Praise those who are obviously connected in the present moment and not day-dreaming.

2. Remind children of last week's poem and ask a pupil to read it out again. Recall the dialogue and take any further comments or evidence from children.

3. Read the story 'The Butterfly'.

4. Ask pupils to remember three things that happened in the story but in reverse chronological order. After giving time for them to do this, let them share these with a partner.

5. Ask children what they thought was the theme of the story. Take answers and build up an ideas web on the board.

6. Move to using the 'Questions for Thinking' to stimulate dialogue.

7. For a closure activity, look again at the web on the board and see which idea or ideas have been developed through the dialogue, and how they have developed.

8. Discuss the 'Thought for the Week'.

Ella goes on a magical exploration to all parts of the world, but will she find what she is looking for . . . ?

THE BUTTERFLY

Ella had once been happy but now she sat, her knees under her chin and her head in her hands, crying.

'What's the matter?' said a voice.

She looked up to see a small green man standing there. There was genuine concern in his three eyes.

Ella wiped away the tears with the back of her hand and tried to smile. 'Are you an alien?' she asked.

The little man smiled too. 'Do I look like a human?'

She shook her head.

'Why were you weeping? Have you lost something?'

Ella nodded. 'Happiness,' she said. 'I had it once but now it's gone and I don't know where to find it.'

'What does it look like?' asked the alien. 'How big is it? What colour is it? If you gave me an idea I could try to help.'

Ella thought for a moment. 'I've never actually seen it,' she said. 'But I know I had it once and now I've lost it. It must be invisible I suppose.'

The alien sighed with impatience. 'Do other people have it?'

'Some do,' replied Ella.

'Then ask them where they got it,' said the little green man. 'It's as simple as that.'

'You're no help,' said Ella. 'I'll have to look for it myself. It must be in a difficult place to find.'

'I didn't see any sign of it when I landed just now,' said the man. 'It's not in the sky. Maybe you should try looking in the sea.'

A brightly coloured butterfly hovered about Ella's face but she jumped to her feet, frightening it away.

'Good idea,' she said. 'I'll go and look in the sea.'

She searched the ocean from one side to the other. She looked in underwater caves and dived among the brilliant fish and orange anemones on the coral reefs. She rode on the backs of dolphins and explored sunken wrecks, but nowhere could she find happiness.

At last Ella climbed ashore and flopped onto the sand. The alien stood there beside his space ship and looked at her expectantly.

'Did you find it?' he asked, but she shook her head.

'No sign of it.'

'Is it a sort of treasure?' asked the alien.

'I suppose it is.'

'Perhaps it's in the old castle over there,' suggested the alien.

A coloured butterfly hung in the air just above her head but Ella jumped up. 'I'll go and see.'

She ran to the old castle and went in through its huge gate. She looked in the dungeons first as that seemed the most obvious place to keep treasure. They were dark and damp and empty. Then she ran around the battlements and up the spiral stone stairs into the tower.

Through the turrets she looked down into the grassy courtyard where children were laughing and playing. There was happiness!

Church bells began to ring and Ella looked down and saw a bride and groom emerging from a church. There was happiness! It was here, all around her. She stood for a moment, watching as people threw handfuls of coloured confetti over the couple. From the corner of her eye she saw another splash of colour, hovering just above her shoulder. As she turned and ran for the stairs, the butterfly was blown over the castle wall, where it landed on the bride's head among the confetti.

Ella arrived panting in the courtyard but the children had gone. Only the little green man stood there, his three eyes looking at her.

'I nearly found it!' exclaimed Ella. 'At least, I saw some people who had it.'

The alien sat down on the grass and put his head in his hands to think.

'Maybe it is guarded by a fierce animal,' he said at last. 'Can you think where that could be?'

'The jungle!' Ella said. 'That's full of fierce animals.'

So off she went and searched through all the biggest and darkest jungles. She risked her life creeping into the dens of lions and the nests of snakes and the river homes of crocodiles, but all to no avail.

Exhausted, she arrived home again and sat on a grassy bank by a stream, and closed her eyes.

'No luck?' asked a voice.

'No,' said Ella.

'Well, I tried,' said the alien. 'I'm off home now. Good luck in your search.'

He climbed into his space ship and Ella heard the whirr of the motor as he zoomed up into the sky.

'I'm not searching any more,' said Ella to herself. 'I'm too tired.'

She lay back and closed her eyes in the cool shade of a tree. A pretty coloured butterfly hovered about for a moment or two before landing on her hand. Ella was too tired to move but she did open her eyes to see what it was.

The butterfly stood, its delicate wings gently moving, and Ella gazed at it in awe.

Then she looked beyond it to the stream, sparkling in the sunshine and she listened to the birds above her in the trees. She took a deep breath and smelt the soft perfume of the flowers and a smile spread across her face.

She felt really happy.

QUESTIONS FOR THINKING

1. What kinds of things make you happy? Who would like to share some things with us?

2. Ella was looking for happiness. Can you remember where she looked for it? (The sea, an old castle, the jungle)

3. In what way did Ella look for happiness?

4. Was there anything wrong with the way Ella looked for happiness? (As if it was an object. This is difficult and may need some 'scaffolding' i.e. clues to assist thinking if necessary).

5. If happiness is not an 'object', what kind of thing is it?

6. Who can describe what Ella learned about happiness?

7. How do you know when you're happy?

8. What stops us being happy?

9. Can you measure happiness? How do you measure it?

10. Can you choose to be happy? How? If you think we can, why don't we choose this all the time?

Thought for the Week

Ella looked for happiness everywhere, thinking it was something outside that she had to find. She finally found it was something inside of her, which was there all the time. Remember that if happiness is inside you, perhaps you can choose to be happy any time you wish. See what can you discover about this during the week.

Block 1 • Session 4

'The Pied Piper' Teaching Notes

Before the lesson copy one set of 'Character Cards' and one set of 'Statements' for each group of 4 or 5 children, and put into group envelopes.

1. Practise the exercise in focusing attention.

2. Recall the story from last week and see if children have evidence of further thinking on the theme, especially in connection with the 'Thought for the Week'.

3. Listen to the story 'The Pied Piper'.

4. Tell the children they are going to get an envelope with 'Character Cards' and 'Statements' by different people. The first task is to match the correct statements to each character. (This is essentially the question, 'Who said What?') To do this the children must all agree before placing a statement with a character so dialogue must take place. It is important to have reasons for placing a statement with a particular character. Give time for this - perhaps 10 or 15 minutes.

5. If some groups are struggling, give them the 'Agree/Disagree/Can't Decide' strategy so they can deal with statements they all agree on before returning to discuss the others.

6. Get each group to report back on only one of the characters, giving the statements and their reasons for including them with that character. (The next group takes a different character, and so on). During the report back, anyone not in the group reporting back may challenge at any time. The person says, 'I challenge that because . . . . ', and gives their evidence for putting the statement with another character. The class may then decide which they think is the best evidence and where the statement should be placed.

7. The Critical Question. 'Using the evidence from your discussions and the report-back, who do you think was the most reasonable - the mayor or the Pied Piper?' Have a short (5-10mins) class dialogue on this question.

8. Creative Thinking. 'Can you think of other possible solutions to the problem?' short dialogue (5-10mins). Try to draw out detail and get children to think through their ideas.

9. Close by praising individuals or groups who have shown good thinking, been focused on their work, and so on.

THE PIED PIPER

A German Folktale

In northern Germany there is a town called Hamelin on the banks of the river Weser. This story took place about seven hundred years ago. The town folk were hard working and honest and lived happily in their grey stone houses, until the rats came.

There had always been rats in the town, as there are in any town, but the cats took care of them so they were no problem.

Suddenly, though, the rats began to multiply. Soon the cats could not keep up with the huge number of rats.

A hundred rats became a thousand. A thousand rats became ten thousand. There were rats everywhere, running in and out of buildings, swarming down the streets. Everywhere you looked were rats.

The people became very worried. Then they became terrified. The rats got into their store houses and barns and ate all the food. They nibbled and chomped their way through everything and became very fat. They became very brave too and sometimes attacked people.

The town council thought about what to do. What they needed was an army of cats, but where would they get so many? They tried putting down poison but that didn't help. They just didn't know what to do. People had nothing to eat. It was a disaster.

The mayor sat with his head in his hands. The once rich and peaceful town had become a place of sadness, filth and starvation.

Then there was a knock on the door.

'Who can that be?' said the councillors. They were a little afraid as they knew that the people were getting angry because nothing was being done.

The knock came again and at last one of the councillors got up and went to answer it.

Outside stood a tall man dressed in strange clothes. His tunic and pants were half yellow and half red and on his head was a grand hat with a feather stuck in it. He held a silver pipe in one hand.

'Good afternoon,' he said, taking off his hat with a flourish. 'I hear that you have a problem with rats. For a thousand florins I will get rid of them once and for all.'

The councillor ushered him in to speak to the mayor.

'A thousand florins!' said the mayor. 'We shall pay it gladly if you can rid our town of this plague.'

So the man left and later could be heard playing his pipe. The thin reedy sound floated into the town hall where the mayor and his councillors still sat, unable to believe that the stranger could do what he said.

But from out of the houses poured the rats, tumbling over each other in frantic haste to follow the piper. Down the street they came in a great black river, paws scrabbling, whiskers twitching, squeaking noisily.

They followed the piper as he walked, playing a tune on his silver pipe. Down to the river they went, and into the swirling waters where they all drowned.

That night the people rejoiced. They could hardly believe they were free of that terrible vermin.

The next morning the piper arrived at the town hall to collect his fee of one thousand florins.

'A thousand florins!' said the mayor. 'That's far too much. We'll give you fifty and that's all. The rats are gone now and they won't come back.'

The piper was angry. 'You'll regret going back on your promise,' he said.

That night the people of Hamelin slept soundly, happy to be free of the rats. Only the children heard the reedy sound of the piper playing on his pipe.

They got out of their beds and dressed and went outside. They followed the piper through the streets, dancing and laughing happily.

Through the woods they went until they reached a mountain and there the piper stopped in front of a high rock. All at once the rock slid open and the piper went in followed by the laughing happy band of children. As the last one entered, the rock door closed so that no-one could see that there had ever been a door there at all.

The children of Hamelin were gone forever, all except one disabled boy.

He could not walk as fast as the others and had got to the mountain too late.

The next morning he told the people what had happened.

It was many years before the laughter and chatter of other children could be heard in Hamelin. And the disabled boy lived the whole of his life regretting that he had not gone with the others, for the piper had told them of the wonderful land where he was taking them.

Townspeople	Mayor
Councillors	Pied Piper
Children	

'I'm really worried about all these rats. If I don't get this problem solved I won't be elected again.'	'This used to be a really clean town. It's disgusting that it's overrun with rats.'
'Let's shake hands on the deal. A thousand florins. That's cheap at the price.'	'I couldn't believe my eyes. From my shop window there was just a river of rats following the piper.'
'That's far too much to pay him. I'll offer him fifty.'	'All of us in this town are honest and hard working.'
'I'll do well in the next election now that I've got rid of the rats.'	'We are all starving. Someone has to do something about this.'
'I think I've kept my part of the bargain.'	'We've got nowhere to play. There's rats everywhere.'
'I've never been to Hamelin before.'	'My ball rolled under the steps. When I went to get it I found a huge black rat gnawing at it.'
'Don't these people realise the power of music?'	'We were all so happy as we skipped along the road.'
'You'll regret going back on your promise.'	'The door just seemed to close behind us.'
'It's our job to solve the problem. The mayor has called a special meeting tomorrow afternoon.'	'I'll do that when I'm finished.'
'The people of our town are starving. If we don't do something about this, it will be the end of us all.'	'This is the first big problem our town has had.'
'They will blame us.'	'There's no laughter in our town anymore.'
'The townspeople will be so pleased with us if this plan works.'	'I didn't know what it all meant.'

Block 1 • Session 5

'Whose Horse' Teaching Notes

1. Remind children that when in the exercise they are connecting with the 'present moment' through the sense of sight, that 'shapes' are not just geometric shapes, but the shapes of anything and everything that can be observed - people, furniture etc, etc. Practise the exercise, then ask what was observed.

2. Read the story 'Whose Horse?'

3. To see who has been listening well, play 'True, False, Can't Tell'. In this, the teacher reads a series of statements about the *content* of the story and pupils have to decide if they are true, or false, or if there is no evidence for their decisions. (If you want to make a bit of fun, let children show their decision in different ways. For example, true by putting hands on heads, false by . . .)

4. Working in pairs, get the children to decide on a theme for the story. Some of these can be put on the board, with lines joining linked ideas.

5. Move to the 'Questions for Thinking' to begin the dialogue.

6. To close, ask for volunteers to sum up the ideas that have been discussed. Let several children do this, with each adding one thought.

WHOSE HORSE?

A Turkish Folk Tale

One day the king decided that he would travel round his country in disguise so that he could see how his people really lived. Mounted on his fine horse, he had almost reached the town of Bassora when he met a poor old beggar by the side of the road.

'Please give me some money!' pleaded the beggar, so the king gave him a coin. Then he asked, 'Where are you going?'

'To Bassora,' said the old man.

'I shall be happy to offer you a ride,' said the king. He got off his horse and helped the old man onto it. Then he mounted behind.

When they reached Bassora, the king asked him to dismount.

'Dismount yourself,' said the beggar. 'The horse is mine!'

'But I gave you a lift!' said the king. 'It is my horse.'

'True,' said the beggar, 'but can you prove it? It is your word against mine.'

The king did not know what to do. If he threw the beggar off into the gutter a crowd would gather and shout at him for stealing the beggar's horse. If he paid the beggar a lot of money to buy the horse back, it would encourage him to steal in future. At last he decided to ask the Judge to settle the case.

In front of them were an oil merchant and a driver.

'Your Honour,' said the oil merchant. 'That coin is mine. I have carried it round for years. I lost it today.'

'Are there any witnesses?' asked the Judge.

'No, your Honour.'

'Then leave the coin with me and return tomorrow,' said the Judge.

Now came the turn of the king and the beggar.

'What is your trouble?' asked the Judge.

'Your Honour,' said the king, 'I am a traveller from a distant land. I took pity on this beggar and gave him a ride but he repays me by demanding that the horse is his.'

'The horse is mine,' said the beggar, pretending to cry, 'I raised him from a colt and we love each other like brothers.'

'Have you any witnesses?' asked the Judge.

'No your Honour,' said the king and the beggar.

'Then leave the horse with me and come back tomorrow,' said the Judge.

So the following morning they both arrived at the courthouse. In front of them were the oil merchant and the driver.

The Judge handed the coin to the oil merchant. 'This is yours,' he said. 'You said that you always carried it in your pocket so I threw it into a glass of water. Soon the surface was covered with tiny bubbles of oil. It must, therefore belong to you.'

Next the king and the beggar came before him. The Judge had the horse brought in and then he handed the reins to the king.

'This is your horse,' he said.

The king nodded. 'It is indeed, your Honour. But how did you know?'

'Last night I had your horse out in a stable which you would pass when you arrived this morning,' said the Judge. 'I was at the stable and when the beggar passed it did not even raise its head. When you passed it stretched out its head and neighed in recognition. Very simple, you see.'

'Your wisdom is beyond compare!' declared the king, taking off his disguise. 'I am the king and I need someone like you in the capital. A wise and honest Judge.'

And so the Judge was rewarded and given a very high position at the grand law courts of the capital city.

QUESTIONS FOR THINKING

1. Why might it have been difficult for the King to react (stop and speak) to the beggar?

2. The King thought that if he threw the beggar off the horse a large crowd might gather and shout at him. What does this tell us about the King? (Make sure children look for as many as possible).

3. What were the examples of justice in the story?

4. Can you think of any other way of being able to work out to whom the horse belonged? If the correct decision was made by another method, would it still have been justice?

5. What is justice?

6. Is there justice in this school? What's your evidence?

7. Are you a just person? What makes you one, or doesn't make you one?

8. Are there any examples of wisdom in the story?

9. Are you wise? Where? How?

10. What is the connection (if any) between wisdom and justice?

Thought for the Week

Look for examples of justice during the week. These may be at home, at school, in the paper, and so on.

Block 1 • Session 6

'I Wake Up' Teaching Notes

1. Do the calming exercise. Take observations from children about what they saw, felt and heard, and praise those whose comments show they were 'in the present' - not day-dreaming.

2. Remind the children of the story 'Whose Horse?' and see if anyone has had more thoughts or observations about justice.

3. Introduce the poem by asking children how they usually feel when they wake up. Read 'I Wake Up' by Michael Rosen. Ask children to listen to the sound of the words, then read it again.

4. Give out copies of the poem and allow pupils to read the poem themselves, then in pairs with each person taking a turn to say it out loud.

5. Still working in pairs, ask the children to discuss together a possible theme. They should formulate reasons for their choice.

6. Build an ideas web on the board (see bibliography) as children give their themes and reasons.

7. Use the 'Questions for Thinking' to begin to build a dialogue.

8. As the dialogue is coming to an end, ask the children to voice what for them is the most important thing they have learned about themselves today.

9. Discuss the 'Thought for the Week.'

I Wake Up

I wake up
I am not me
I am bodyless
I am weightless
I am legless
I am armless
I am in the sea of my mind
I am in the middle of my brain
I am afloat in a sea of nothing

It lasts for one flicker
Of one eyelash

and then
once again
I am my full heaviness
I am my full headedness
I am my full bodyness
Here.
Hello.

Michael Rosen
(Quick Let's Get Out of Here)

50

QUESTIONS FOR THINKING

1. What is the poet describing?

2. This is not our usual way of waking up. Have you ever felt like this just at the instant that you wake up? (If some have, let them recall it, as accurately as possible).

3. What does '. . . in the sea of my mind . . . in the middle of my brain . . . in a sea of nothing' mean? What is being described?

4. Where do you think the poet's body was at this time? Why did he give the description?

5. What do you think happens when he becomes heavy again? (See footnote).

6. Who is '. . . in the sea of my mind . . . in the middle of my brain . . . afloat in a sea of nothing?'

7. Ask yourself 'Who am I?' What is the answer? Are you your name? Are you your body? Are you your mind? Who are you?

8. Who or what was it that noticed that it was 'bodyless, weightless, legless, and so on?

Footnote: The process of waking up 'cleanly' i.e. not dozing/dreaming, is one of cognition - recognition - memory, as Michael Rosen describes in the poem. Children are more likely to experience this than adults (for various reasons) so keep an open mind and see what comes from discussion. The 'becoming heavy again' is at the recognition/memory stage when consciousness is 'attached' to the body again i.e. I know I have a body and am not just conscious.

Thought for the Week

Try to notice how you wake up. Is it different at different times? Is it ever like the poet describes? If so, does it help you understand the poem more fully?

Block 1 • Session 7

'The Blind Men and the Elephant' Teaching Notes

1. Practise the exercise in focusing and calming.

2. Recall last week's session and have someone read the poem 'I Wake Up', again. See if anyone has noticed anything about waking up that relates to the poem, and discuss anything significant.

3. Introduce and read 'The Blind Men and the Elephant'.

4. Get children to make up three questions about the story and then in groups of three or four, ask each other the questions.

5. Give thinking time so that everyone can consider what they think is the main point of the story. In the same small groups, share the ideas, giving reasons for their choices. Children can question or 'challenge' if they think someone's evidence is not very robust.

6. Ask each group to choose what they think is the best idea, then put these forward to the class. Note these on the board. With everyone's attention on the five or six ideas gathered, ask pupils how it would be possible to change each one into a philosophical question. (If necessary, remind children of the nature of a philosophical question). One by one, write down the questions that emerge from the ideas.

7. Stimulate the dialogue using the 'Questions for Thinking'.

8. For a closure to the session, let the group collectively trace the route of the dialogue. (That is, what were the ideas at the beginning, how did they develop and change, and what was the finishing position?)

9. Discuss the 'Thought for the Week'.

How often do we think we know about something, only to find we only had partial knowledge? Trouble arises when we have made decisions based on our partial knowledge. This traditional story from India illustrates this in a humorous way.

THE BLIND MEN AND THE ELEPHANT

Long ago, in India, there lived six men who had all been blind since birth. Often they would meet and sit in the shade of a tree to talk about their experiences and one day the subject of discussion was the elephant. None of them knew what it looked like, of course, but they had heard many stories of this great beast.

One day they heard that a rich man who owned an elephant was to visit a nearby village so they travelled there and asked him if they could each investigate the elephant. The rich man was happy to show off his possession and led the first blind man up to the great beast.

The first man tripped over a rock and fell against the elephant's side, putting out his hands to save himself. He felt the thick rough skin as far as he could reach.

'Oh,' he said. 'It's like a great wall.'

The second man went forward, his hands outstretched. The elephant had turned slightly and the first thing the man touched was its tusks.

'It's long and hard and smooth,' he said. 'Just like a spear.'

The third man stepped towards the elephant a little to the rear and grabbed its tail.

'No,' he said. 'It's coarse and pliable like a thick rope.'

It was the turn of the fourth man.

He reached out and touched the trunk.

'It is long and squirms and wriggles like a snake,' he said, as the elephant wrapped it around his waist.

Then came the fifth man, who touched the animal's ear.

'No,' he muttered in awe. 'I feel one of its wings here. It is a flying animal.'

Finally the sixth man stepped forward, intrigued by what his friends had said. Now, at last, he would know for himself. He touched one of the legs. He felt it up and down and side to side.

'You are all wrong,' he said. 'It is like the trunk of a stout palm tree.'

The six blind men went back to the shade of their tree to discuss - and argue - about their experiences. All thought they were right, since they had felt the elephant for themselves.

QUESTIONS FOR THINKING

1. Why do you think this story is told? What is the lesson that can be learned from it? (Full knowledge of something is better than partial knowledge).

2. At the start, the men didn't have any knowledge about an elephant. How did they begin to get some knowledge? How do we get knowledge of something?

3. Each of the men had a little knowledge about an elephant. Why is it important to have as much knowledge of a situation as possible?

4. Can you think of times when you have made decisions with only partial knowledge?

5. Can we always rely on the knowledge we have of something? Can you think of any occasions when we couldn't rely on information?

6. What does the word 'knowledge' mean?

7. What is knowledge?

8. What use is knowledge? Do we need it? Why or why not?

9. Where does knowledge come from? Are there different kinds of knowledge?

10. Often when we get knowledge of something, we make decisions based on that. What happens to our decision making when we only have partial knowledge of something?

11. What has philosophy or a 'community of enquiry' got to do with knowledge?

Thought of the Week

It is easy to get ourselves into trouble when we make decisions based on partial knowledge. During the week try to see whether you think you have good evidence before believing things. Try to have as much knowledge of a situation as possible before making decisions.

Block 1 • Session 8

'The Boy Who Cried Wolf' Teaching Notes

Before the lesson, copy one set of 'Character Cards' and one set of 'Statements' for each group of 4 or 5 children. Cut them out and put into envelopes, one per group.

1. Practise the exercise. Ask children what they noticed going on in their mind. For example, did they drift off into daydreams for long periods or were they able to stay quite focused. (It takes close observation to recognise this). Praise those who had good attention.

2. Recall the story 'The Blind Men and the Elephant' and ask if children had realised anything during the week about having good evidence and speaking from knowledge rather than partial knowledge.

3. Tell the children they are going to do another critical challenge today, then read them 'The Boy Who Cried Wolf'.

4. Remind pupils that the first task is to match the statements with the characters, but that they can only match a statement with a character when the whole group agrees with the decision. They must have reasons for their decisions. Give 10 to 15 minutes for this.

5. If you are assessing one group with the 'Matrix for Critical Thinking', stay with that group, otherwise move around groups, scaffolding if necessary.

6. Get each group to report back on one of the characters, giving the statements and their reasons for including them with that character. (The next group takes a second character, and so on). During the report back, anyone may challenge at anytime. The challenger must give their reasons for placing the information with another character. The class can decide the best evidence and where the statement should be placed.

7. The Critical Question, the wise man said, 'A liar will not be believed, even when he speaks truth.' Do you think this is true? Have a short (5-10 mins) class dialogue on this question.

8. Creative Thinking. Brainstorm the question, 'What else could David have done to stop getting bored?'

9. Do the exercise for a minute, just concentrating on listening.

10. Discuss the 'Thought for the Week.'

THE BOY WHO CRIED WOLF

Aesop's Fable

David was a shepherd who looked after sheep in pastures at the foot of a mountain. All day he sat and watched the flock, making sure none strayed and got lost or were caught by wolves. In summer he sat and dozed a little in the shade of a great oak tree and in winter he huddled over a fire with the mountain at his back to shelter him from the cold wind.

Soon he became rather bored with his job. It was so quiet and the sheep were no company. If he spoke to them they ignored him and didn't answer but just quietly chewed at the grass.

One day David thought of a plan. A way to cause a bit of excitement.

He ran down the field towards the village shouting. 'Wolf! Wolf!'

The villagers came running out of their houses, some carrying weapons to frighten the wolves away. They spread all over the mountain side looking for wolves and some stayed with him for a while.

David enjoyed the company.

A few days later he tried the same thing again, and then again. Soon the villagers realised that there were no wolves about at all.

'You are wasting our time,' they told David. 'And you are lying too. You know there are no wolves about.'

But one day, as David sat under the oak tree, the sheep suddenly became restless. They bleated and scurried about nervously. David got up and shaded his eyes to see what was wrong.

At the edge of the flock crept a dark shape. It was a wolf!

At once David fled down the field towards the village.

'Wolf! Wolf!' he cried.

But this time the villagers ignored him.

'Wolf! Wolf!' yelled David again.

But the villagers took no notice. They were not going to be fooled again by this lying boy.

And so some of David's sheep were killed by the wolf and he complained to the wise man of the village.

The wise man said, 'A liar will not be believed, even when he speaks the truth.'

David the Shepherd	**Villagers**
Wise Man	**Farmer**
David's **Mother**	

He's always been a lazy boy. His father was always getting on to him about helping around the house.	I wish he'd worked harder at school.
I'm so ashamed that he's caused so much trouble.	What will I do with that boy?
No matter what, I'll still love him.	Our actions always have consequences.
Be careful what you say - it always has a result.	You must be responsible for your actions.
A liar will not be believed, even when he speaks truth.	My advice is that you should apologise for wasting people's time.
The stupid boy has lost me some of my sheep.	Sheep are expensive.
I'll need to get a new shepherd.	Wolves are a danger to farmers.
It's hard enough to make a living, without something like this happening.	In my job sometimes you get a bit bored and lonely.
How can I make life more exciting?	I know all the sheep by name and their habits.
I'm going to complain about lack of help.	I really enjoy some company sometimes.
Quick, come to help, there's a wolf up on the hillside.	I'm beginning to be suspicious, have you ever seen one?
I tell you Bob, if it happens again ignore it.	We work well together and always help each other out.

Block 1 • Session 9

'A Thing of Beauty' Teaching Notes

1. Do the calming exercise by asking the children to focus particularly on listening. Afterwards, take examples of what was heard. Praise those examples that show that the child was focused on the sense impressions and not on any interpretation - that is, thinking about them.

2. Introduce the story by asking children if they have noticed anything beautiful lately. Read 'A Thing of Beauty'.

3. Ask two or three factual questions to make sure the content was understood.

4. Give the children time to think of three events contained in the story, and the ideas that link them. In pairs, share this information.

5. Let a number of children report back to the class. Praise those who speak particularly well, for example, at length with good evidence, with creative ideas, with linked ideas.

6. Begin the dialogue by using the 'Questions for Thinking'.

7. For a closure activity, ask children to reveal their question/theme and draw any connections (if possible) between what is written and any elements that have emerged in the dialogue. Take examples.

8. Discuss the 'Thought for the Week'.

Molly kicked at a stone on the path and sent it skittering into the grass. She didn't want to be here. Here was boring. Here was the camping holiday with her parents and pain-in-the-neck brother Nicky. A whole week of nothing to do while her friends - not to mention Josh - had gone to Scotland with the school trip.

They were probably having a great time, she hardly dared think of it. She could cry with frustration when she thought of who Josh might be sitting next to on the coach.

Well, one thing was for sure - he wouldn't be thinking of her! He wouldn't have time to think about her and with girls out numbering boys, what chance did she have of still being his girlfriend after the holidays?

Had her parents considered that? Did they understand just what it meant to be Josh Bentine's girl? She, Molly Anderson, with mousy hair and fat legs? She wasn't exactly someone the boys fought over.

Molly scuffed along, raising dust which settled on her white trainers - but she didn't care. Somewhere back there they would be getting up and making breakfast and wondering where she was. Let them wonder. Let them worry. They'd soon wish they had let her go on the school trip. She'd be miserable the whole week, spoil their holiday as they had spoilt her life.

She had lost Josh for sure.

Her toe caught on a rock embedded in the path and before she could regain her balance she was over, crashing down onto the grass at the side of the path. She fell hard onto her hip and lay there for a moment, eyes screwed up until the initial pain subsided. Now, on top of everything else, she would have a nice colourful bruise.

Molly opened her eyes but made no attempt to get up. She felt thoroughly fed up. She stared up at the sky, blue with a few high streaky clouds.

Something tickled her cheek and she turned her head to one side to see what it was. In front of her eyes was something bright yellow. She stared at the glorious colour, at the petals with frayed ends arranged in circles, darker orange in the centre. The petals were of uneven length yet the whole flower had a pleasing symmetry.

It was just a common dandelion. A weed. Yet now it looked so beautiful. She had never really looked closely at a flower before, and certainly not a dandelion. Why should just a weed be so lovely? Weeds were nuisance plants. People pulled them up and threw them away.

Slowly, Molly got to her feet and looked around her. There were dandelions everywhere like a golden carpet and in amongst them other flowers and grass. Beyond that the ground sloped away and she could see the sun glinting on a stream, way down in the valley. Beyond that the hills rose again.

Molly turned around. Behind her a dry-stone wall meandered over the brow of the hill, broken in places, blotchy grey with lichen. Here and there small plants sprouted from between the stones.

The sun was growing warmer and Molly turned her face towards it and took a deep breath. She was suddenly aware of birds twittering in a nearby tree as if she'd had the sound turned off and had just turned up the volume.

It was really beautiful here. She longed to run down to the stream and paddle in the cool water. Feeling really hungry she turned back along the track, not scuffing her feet now but almost running.

The breeze ruffled her hair and she shook it behind her. Suddenly she felt beautiful. Josh had said he loved her hair. Wasn't there more to a person than what they looked like? You had to look deep inside to see other kinds of beauty - like the dandelion. Even weeds were beautiful.

Josh had said he would ring her and she had left her mobile in the tent.

Molly began to run.

QUESTIONS FOR THINKING

1. What describes Molly's state at the start of the story?

2. What were the causes?

3. Were the causes real or imaginary?

4. What does 'real' mean in this example?

5. Is beauty real? How do you know? What is real about it?

6. What began to happen to Molly after she had tripped up? (Her attention moved from being on ideas in her head to the world [beauty] around her). Further question the initial replies of the children.

7. What changed when Molly moved her attention from her worries to the beauty around her?

8. Is there a link between beauty and happiness? If so, what is it?

9. If there is a link, is there *always* a link, and is it always the same link?

10. Sometimes we think something is beautiful and at other times the same thing appears to be not beautiful - or it is not noticed at all. Does the beautiful thing change or is it something else that changes? (This may take some questioning and investigation to make clear).

11. Exactly what is it that changes?

12. Sometimes we can be surrounded by beauty and not notice it. Why is that? (An example may be useful - walking through a beautiful park and not being very aware of it).

Thought for the Week

See what examples of beauty you can see during the week. Ask yourself what is real about them. Notice how you feel at the time.

Block 1 • Session 10

'Spotlight on Smoking' Teaching Notes

1. Do the calming exercise.

2. Ask children if they have had further thoughts about beauty. How did they feel? Was the beauty real?

3. Tell the children they are going to use a magazine article for a stimulus this week. They will be trying to identify any philosophical issues in the story and frame some philosophical questions. Read 'Spotlight on Smoking'.

4. Ask children some questions to determine that they have understood the story.

5. Remind children of the nature of philosophical questions. (If necessary give them a strategy such as first identifying a theme, then formulating a question. E.g. If the theme of the story was 'fear', one question would be 'What is fear?') Give time for them to consider the article and think about different themes. They should have reasons for their choice.

6. Share questions and reasons in pairs.

7. Build a web of questions on the board and show any link or tensions between the ideas given. Children should give their reasons as they give their questions.

8. Review the range of ideas given, then give pupils time to consider all the ideas and choose the one they would like to investigate further through enquiry. Take a vote to determine the question to begin the dialogue.

9. Ask the person who originally put forward the idea to start the dialogue by re-stating the question and putting forward their own view.

10. In building the enquiry, remember to use a variety of types of question such as suggested in the 'Questions for Thinking' section at the beginning of this book. If the enquiry 'runs out of steam', go to the question with the second number of votes, and so on.

SPOTLIGHT ON SMOKING

'I have made it a rule never to smoke more than one cigar at a time. I have no other restriction as regards smoking. I do not know just when I began to smoke. I only know that it was in my father's lifetime and he died in 1847, when I was eleven. As an example to others, and not that I care for moderation myself, it has always been my practice never to smoke when asleep and never to refrain when awake. Today it is all over sixty years since I began smoking to the limit.' **Mark Twain (on his 70th birthday in 1905)**

Tobacco was first introduced in Britain around 1585 by Sir Walter Raleigh on his return from Virginia, USA. It was prohibited then, by priests and rulers, especially James I, but to no avail. From that day on people have smoked it in pipes, cigars and cigarettes, chewed it and sniffed it (snuff).

Nowadays, according to the Cancer Research Campaign, more children are starting to smoke than adults. In 1988, 8% of children between 11 and 15 smoked. In 1996 it had risen to 13%. Now one in four 15 year olds smoke.

Although, as you see above, not everyone who smokes will die of cancer or a related illness. (Only 50%, according to Government statistics). Many smokers will tell you their grandfather or aunt smoked all their life and died at 101. It's a risk, just like sky-diving or crossing the road. And they warn you on the packet, don't they? Why can't you make the choice? It's your life.

Why do we smoke? Well, it's cool to smoke. Everyone does it. It's more fun because it's not allowed. It makes us feel grown-up. It gives us a buzz. You have to experience everything.

Never mind that we'll get addicted. What does it matter if we smell like an old ash tray and our teeth go yellow? Who cares if we get a cough and are ill with bronchitis every year. We can't think about when we're old and might get cancer.

But wait . . . on a recent advertising campaign they showed people in their 30's dying of lung cancer.

Smoking is expensive. Just think what you could do with all that money going up in smoke. In a lifetime it could add up to many thousands of pounds. Right now you can plan how you're going to spend the money you save on cigarettes. It's like winning the lottery! And you could be healthy enough to enjoy it too.

People are suing tobacco companies because they blame their illnesses on smoking and say they weren't warned that it was bad for them. Should we be warned of all dangers or should we be able to judge for ourselves?

Think seriously about all that poisonous smoke going into your lungs.

Are you prepared to take the risk?

BLOCK TWO

In this block, the following thinking skills have a particular focus in the pair/group work;

Theme to Philosophical Question

A strong emphasis has been placed throughout the term on reinforcing and consolidating the ability to determine a theme from the stimulus, then turn it into a philosophical question.

Block 2 • Session 1

'It's Not Fair' Teaching Notes

1. Remind children of the reasons for doing the calming exercise. Reinforce the importance of being actively 'connected' through the senses - not just sitting being quiet. Talk the class through the exercise.

2. As it is the start of a new block of work, ask children to recall the rules of good dialogue that have been previously agreed upon.

3. Introduce the story 'It's Not Fair', and read it.

4. Ask the class to think of three things that they think are important that happened in the story. Give time for them to do this.

5. In pairs or threes, pupils should share ideas and give reasons for their choices. Once this has been done, it can be done as a class, with the main ideas being written up on the board.

6. Draw any links (both metaphorically and on the board), between ideas, and also show ideas opposed to each other - perhaps in a different colour.

7. Move to the dialogue, using the 'Questions for Thinking' as aids.

8. Discuss the 'Thought for the Week'.

'It's not fair!' How often do we hear children saying or whining that? Fairness is the basis of Justice, and is especially close to the hearts of children. It is important that things are fair, that children are treated fairly, and that they see that things are fair. 'That's not fair', can however become a habitual response when things don't suit the child, and in that circumstance, have nothing to do with fairness. It is important that children do examine issues objectively to see if they really are fair or not.

IT'S NOT FAIR

'It's not fair!' said Maddy, between bites of her sandwich. 'Mum and Dad going to Paris without us.'

'Well, that's a fine thing,' said her Uncle Ted with a grin. 'And we thought you liked staying with us.'

'Oh, we do,' said Maddy. 'But we've never been to Paris, and we could have gone to Disneyland. Do you think Mum and Dad will go there?'

Uncle Ted shook his head. 'There are plenty of other things to see in Paris,' he said.

After lunch the four of them went to the beach. Maddy, her brother Joe, Uncle Ted and Auntie Barbara. Not forgetting Jess, their Labrador.

'Let's walk along as far as the pier and back,' said Auntie Barbara. 'See you later, Jess.' She locked the car door, making sure one window was open.

'Why can't Jess come too?' asked Joe.

'Dogs are not allowed on this part of the beach,' said Auntie Barbara.

'That's not fair!' said Joe.

On the pier was a stall selling candy floss and Uncle Ted bought some for each of the children. 'Special treat,' he said.

That evening the children were tired from their journey and the long walk. At eight o'clock Auntie Barbara said, 'I think it's time you both went to bed.'

As they went upstairs Maddy yawned and said, 'It's not fair! I usually stay up later than Joe because I'm older.'

'Look at you, you're tired,' said Auntie Barbara. 'Have a good sleep and we'll have another nice day tomorrow.'

Maddy was woken by Jess licking her face. She giggled and got out of bed, her arm round the dog's neck.

'All right, Jess. I'm up.' She looked out of the window and her face fell as she saw the grey clouds and the misty rain falling.

'It's raining!' she complained to Auntie Barbara, sitting at the table and reaching for the glass of orange juice. 'What can we do today?'

Joe was already there. 'We're going to play a game,' he said through a mouthful of cereal.

'What sort of game?' asked Maddy.

'The weather's going to clear up this afternoon,' said Auntie Barbara, stacking the dishes in the dishwasher. 'But I thought we'd play a little game. It's called Justice.'

Both children looked at her. They'd never heard of that game.

'Yesterday,' went on Auntie Barbara, 'you both said that things weren't fair. In fact three times you said, 'It's not fair!'

They giggled at her imitation of them.

'What is fairness?' she asked.

'Being the same for everyone,' said Joe.

'Justice,' said Maddy. 'The name of the game. Not giving someone more than another.'

'Yes,' said their aunt. 'But there's more to it than that. You have to take into account the circumstances as well. You have to look at every aspect. Let's talk about the things you thought were unfair yesterday.'

'Maddy, you said it wasn't fair that your Mum and Dad went to Paris without you, but it's their wedding anniversary, isn't it? Although they love being with you two, don't you think it's nice for them to be together sometimes? After all, you are having a holiday too.'

Maddy nodded.

'Then you Joe,' said their aunt, 'thought it wasn't fair that we couldn't take Jess on the beach. The thing is that not all dogs are well trained by their owners to do their business in the right place. People lie on the beach and children play there too. Dog dirt can spread diseases. There is a part of the beach further away from the town where dogs can go. So that sounds fair, doesn't it?'

Joe nodded.

'Now let's look at what wouldn't have been fair,' said Auntie Barbara. 'What if someone said that as a special favour Jess could go on the beach but other dogs couldn't. That wouldn't be fair. What if Uncle Ted had bought one of you a candy floss and not the other. That wouldn't have been fair, would it?'

'No!' they said together.

'But,' said Auntie Barbara, 'you were right, Maddy, when you said that it wasn't fair for you to go to bed at the same time as Joe. Being older does give you certain privileges and that is perfectly fair because Joe will get them when he is older.'

Joe pouted but nodded his head at the same time.

'So next time you say, 'It's not fair!' play the Justice game. Ask yourself if you are just thinking only from your own point of view or if it is reasonable for everyone.'

'Look! It's stopped raining, ' exclaimed Joe.

Auntie Barbara smiled. 'Fair weather,' she said, 'just as they forecast.'

QUESTIONS FOR THINKING

1. Fairness has to do with Justice. We all like things to be fair. Think of the things that Maddy and Joe thought were not fair. Why did they say they weren't fair?

2. When Aunty Barbara made them think about and examine the things they thought were unfair, the children changed their minds. (Remind children of the issues that were thought unfair). Why did they change their minds?

3. Had the events themselves changed? (The events previously thought unfair). What had changed? (Their point of view).

4. Why had they changed their point of view?

5. When people say 'That's not fair', to whom do they think it's not fair?

6. Is an event ever fair or unfair, or do people make it one or the other? How? Why?

7. Which do you think is best fairness or unfairness? (Justice or injustice?) Why?

8. Is there any time when unfairness would be best? Examples?

9. Is it possible to be fair all the time? What would this mean in practical circumstances?

Thought for the Week

Next time you hear yourself saying (or about to say) 'It's not fair!', play the Justice game and think about all the circumstances around your problem. Check if you're only considering yourself. Do you have all the information? Ask yourself - 'Is it really fair? Am I being Just?'

Block 2 • Session 2

'Responsibility' Teaching notes

1. Practise the exercise.

2. Recall last week's story and discuss whether the children had found any evidence that their actions were 'just' or 'unjust'.

3. Read 'Responsibility', and give out copies so that children have access to one between two.

4. The poem is very short and the implications are quite subtle for children. Allow them, in their pairs, to discuss what the theme of the poem might be, and why the poet might have written it. Move around the class whilst this activity takes place, and 'scaffold' ideas for children if necessary.

5. Use the 'Questions for Thinking' to stimulate dialogue.

6. To close the session, ask children to consider, what for them, has been an important new idea today.

7. Discuss the 'Thought for the Week'.

Responsibility

Each thought I think, each little word I say,
Goes travelling outwards far and away,
And like a bottle drifting on the sea,
None know whereat its landing place will be.

Maud Keary
From 'Enchanted Tulips and Other Verse for Children' (1914)

QUESTIONS FOR THINKING

1. In what ways can words go 'travelling outwards far and far away'?

2. Why does the author talk about bottles drifting on the sea? What has this got to do with words?

3. Can you ever tell where your words will end up? Has anyone any examples?

4. Why do you think the poet wrote the poem?

5. What effects can words have? Have you any examples?

6. Can there be positive as well as negative results? What examples can we think of?

7. Why do you think the poet gave the poem the title that she did?

8. If it is true that we don't know what effects words have, why might this be important to know? Why?

9. Could there be positive as well as negative reasons in question 7, and why?

Thought for the Week

Be aware of what you say, and of any effect it may have. This is a useful way of being sure that you don't hurt people or cause problems without knowing it.

Block 2 • Session 3

'The Mongoose and the Farmer's Wife' Teaching Notes

1. Remind the class that the exercise reinforces and strengthens the ability to give attention, which is related to the ability to learn. Practise the focusing exercise together.

2. Recall the poem from last week and let someone read it out again. Has anyone paid more attention to what they say, and its effects? Discuss any examples.

3. Read the story of 'The Mongoose and the Farmer's Wife'.

4. Ask the children to think about the story and think of four things that happened in the story, in the correct order. They should share these with a partner.

5. Use the 'Questions for Thinking' to begin the dialogue.

6. Make sure the 'Thought for the Week' is fully understood.

A story from the Panchatantra collection of India.

THE MONGOOSE AND THE FARMER'S WIFE

Once upon a time there lived a farmer and his wife. They lived in a small village in southern India, where they worked hard to earn a living from their small farm. This was very difficult as the farm was tiny in comparison to most farms here, but the couple were determined to make the best of life, and hoped to raise a family. After some time they were very pleased when a son was born to them. There were great celebrations in the family, and many villagers came to see the baby and bring him good wishes.

As the baby grew into a toddler, the farmer's wife wanted to have a pet animal to protect the child, and also to be a companion for him. She talked for a long time with her husband and in the end they decided upon a mongoose. A mongoose is a small furry animal found in India, which is about the size and shape of a ferret. It is known for its speed of action and also its ability to kill snakes. Now you might be more used to having a cat or a dog for a pet, but the farmer thought that a mongoose would be a fine pet and he hoped it would take care of the child if his wife had some work to do on the farm.

One day, after going out to collect eggs, the wife returned home to find the mongoose waiting at the door of the house, its mouth stained with blood. She was immediately filled with horror and thought that it had killed or injured her child. In a rage she picked up a box and threw it at the mongoose, hurting it badly. She then rushed through into the baby's room, to find the child sitting happily in his cot. On the floor she was surprised to see a dead snake, its throat deeply bitten, leaving a trail of blood on the floor. Realising that she had made a mistake, and that the mongoose had in fact saved the child, the woman ran back to the other room - only to find the mongoose also dead. Sadly, the farmer's wife sat down on an old wooden kitchen chair and sobbed aloud at her hasty action.

QUESTIONS FOR THINKING

1. Why do you think the farmer's wife chose a mongoose as a pet for her son?

2. What happened in the lady's mind when she first saw the mongoose with its bloodstained mouth?

3. The farmer's wife had made a decision. What was the decision? Did she have good evidence for making her decision?

4. How did the lady feel? What was the cause of her feelings?

5. How do you think she felt when she first saw her son was unharmed? What do you think her next feeling was? Why?

6. Why did the lady cry?

7. What is anger?

8. What causes anger?

9. Does being angry do any good?

10. Is it possible to change actions once they have happened? What does this mean for us?

Thought for the Week

'Jumping to conclusions' can cause lots of problems. Watch to see if you have good evidence for the actions you take.

Block 2 • Session 4

'Beauty and the Beast' Teaching Notes

Before the lesson, copy one set of 'Character Cards' and one set of 'Statements' for each group of 4 or 5 children, and put into group envelopes.

1. Practise the exercise in focusing attention. Remind pupils that there should not be any tension - rather, they should rest in the sharp focus of the present moment.

2. Recall the story about the farmer's wife and the pet mongoose, and see if the children have noticed anything about jumping to conclusions. Discuss any observations.

3. Listen to the story of 'Beauty and the Beast'.

4. Remind children they are going to get an envelope with character cards containing statements by different people. The first task is to match the correct statements to each character - answering the question 'Who said what?' To do this the children must all agree before placing the statement with a character so dialogue must take place. It is important that the children have reasons for placing a statement with a particular character. Give time for this - perhaps 10 or 15 minutes.

5. Should groups struggle to agree, give them the 'Agree/Disagree/Can't Decide' strategy so they can deal with statements they do agree on, before returning to discuss the others.

6. Ask each group to report back on only one of the characters, giving their reasons for including them with that character. The next group takes the next character, and so on. During the report back, anyone not in the group reporting back may challenge at any time. To do so the pupil says 'I challenge that because . . .', and goes on to give evidence as to why they would put the statement with another character. The class can then decide which they think is the stronger evidence and where the statement should be placed.

7. The Critical Question. 'Using the evidence from your discussions and the report back, do you think Bella really loved the beast?' Have a short (5-10 min.) dialogue on this question.

8. Creative Thinking. 'Can you think of any other solutions to the predicament that the merchant found himself in'? Give children time to think, then have a short dialogue on this, examining together any solutions put forward.

BEAUTY AND THE BEAST

There was once a merchant who had three daughters. Just before he set off on a business trip, he asked them what they would like him to bring back for them.

'A necklace please, father,' said the eldest.

'A gold chain for me please,' said the middle daughter.

But the youngest daughter, whose name was Bella, just shook her head.

'I want nothing, father,' she said. 'Just bring yourself back safely.'

'Nonsense,' said their father. 'I want to bring you a gift.'

Bella thought for a moment. 'Then I would like a rose, please.'

The merchant went about his business and he bought the necklace and the gold chain for his two eldest daughters but decided to leave the rose until last so that it would be fresh. Then he forgot about it.

He was almost home when he suddenly remembered the rose and started to look around for somewhere to buy one. As he turned a corner he saw a beautiful garden and there, in the centre of a circle of lawn, was a rose bush laden with blooms.

The merchant got off his horse, walked through the great wrought iron gates and stepped onto the grass circle. Surely the owners wouldn't miss one rose. He chose a deep red rosebud and plucked it off the bush.

CRASH! A loud noise filled his ears and there, in front of him, stood a hideous beast. Its eyes were red and glaring, its lips curled back from a cluster of pointed grey teeth. Three horns protruded from the green scaly skin of its head and long strings of saliva dripped from its black tongue.

'Thief !' growled the beast. 'You are stealing my roses.'

The merchant explained about the gift for his daughter.

'That is no excuse! Your life is forfeit.'

'Oh please,' begged the merchant. 'Please spare my life. I have three daughters to support and care for. I am really sorry for stealing your rose.'

'I shall spare your life on one condition,' said the beast. 'Seven days from now you must bring me your youngest daughter.'

The merchant arrived home to a great welcome from his daughters and gave them their gifts, but the youngest daughter could tell that something was wrong and he was unhappy.   Eventually he told her about the beast and the condition it imposed to spare his life.

'I will go, father,' said Bella, bravely. So the next day they set off.

Like her father, Bella was shocked when she saw the beast and could hardly bare to look at his ugliness. The beast told the merchant that he could visit Bella every week and that he meant her no harm.

Bella was shown to her luxurious rooms and over the next few weeks she had everything she wanted. She only had to ask for something out loud and some invisible servants brought it to her. The beast hardly ever appeared. Bella spent the long days walking in the vast gardens or reading books.

It sounds wonderful, doesn't it? But Bella began to get lonely. Apart from seeing her father or sisters once a week she never saw anyone else at all.

On one of the rare times when the beast appeared, Bella asked him to walk with her in the garden. Then she told him about her father and sisters and of her mother who had died when she was a child.

Bella talked more and more with the beast. He was so kind and thoughtful that she lost her fear of him and the walks in the garden became a daily event that she looked forward to. She told him about her life and her interests and her hopes.

Then one day the beast did not appear. Bella felt really disappointed and she waited an hour before going to look for him. She searched the whole great house, looking in rooms she had never been in before, but she couldn't find the beast.

Then, as she passed an open window, she heard cries and groans of pain coming from the front garden. Down the stairs she ran, through the front door and out to the very rosebush from which her father had plucked the rose. There was the beast, lying on the ground with blood pouring from a great wound in his chest. He was gasping for breath and twisting in agony.

Bella fell on her knees beside him. 'What's happened? Who did this to you?'

'The people of the village,' whispered the beast. 'They think I am evil. They don't like me living here.'

Frantically she tore off a piece of her skirt and tried to staunch the flow of blood.

'Oh please don't die, beast,' she wept. 'Please don't die. I love you so much.'
There was a flash of bright light and suddenly a prince stood before her, his handsome face smiling with love and gratitude.

'You have broken the spell!' he said.

Bella wiped her eyes and stared at him in bewilderment.

'I was enchanted by an evil magician,' explained the prince. 'And the spell could only be broken if a maiden declared her love for me of her own free will. You did that. Ugly as I was, you still loved me.'

Bella and the prince were married and . . .

lived . . . happily . . . ever . . . after!

I saw something beautiful inside of him.	I am imprisoned in this body.
What a person, is, is more important than what they look like.	I am not wicked or hurtful.
I'm not so interested in fancy presents.	Why do people torment me?
I learned that fear could be overcome.	I need someone to recognise what I am really like.
The more knowledge I had, the more I changed my mind.	I long for freedom.
It is my duty to do this.	Thank goodness it wasn't one of us who had to go.
I'm scared of going visiting.	How can we make her life happier?
How could I have put her in such danger?	It's so ugly we must do something about it.
'How could I have exchanged my own life for someone elses?'	It's a threat to our village.
What a fine example she has set - she is a lovely person.	Meet tonight at 8pm in the village square.
How could people be so hurtful and ignorant?	Maybe there's more of them, we'll need to find out.

Merchant	Bella
Beast	Villagers
Sisters	

Block 2 • Session 5

'A Little Wisdom' Teaching Notes

1. Practise the calming and focusing exercise.

2. Introduce the story and read 'A Little Wisdom'.

3. Discuss the concept of 'theme' with the class, and how it is possible to have an 'inner' meaning to a story - like a moral in a traditional fairy tale. In this way this story could be considered in relation to its content and also in relation to a theme.

4. Ask two or three questions about content, then ask children to formulate one. Give time. Then working in pairs, they each ask a partner their question.

5. Ask children to consider what the theme could be, and again give time for this. They should again share this with their partner, this time giving reasons as to why they consider it a main theme.

6. As a class, children should now feedback their ideas so that a web of ideas can be built up on the board. Draw links between similar or linked ideas, and likewise link opposing ideas but in a different colour.

7. Consider, as a class, the range of ideas shown. Linking with the theme in the 'Questions for Thinking', now move to them as an aid to developing the dialogue.

8. At the end of the dialogue, consider again the main ideas from the dialogue as against those on the board. For example, how many were investigated in the enquiry? What was the depth of the investigation.

9. Discuss the 'Thought for the Week', and ensure all understand what to look for.

Many people seem to associate wisdom with age, that somehow life experience and wisdom are the same thing. Mark is no exception, but he begins to see that not only can he be wise, but that so can everyone else.

A LITTLE WISDOM

'I can't be wise,' said Mark.

'Why not?' asked his teacher, Miss Fletcher.

Mark shrugged. He thought of the times he'd heard about being wise. The three wise men. The wise old owl.

'You have to be old,' went on Mark. 'You have to know a lot and have had things happen to you.'

'Well, you're wrong,' said the teacher. 'Anyone can be wise. It's all about thinking things out and making the right decisions, based on your experiences. All you children have had experiences in your short lives. You can be wise in small ways.'

Mark wasn't convinced.

When Miss Fletcher had asked the class to find out what wisdom was Mark was sure it was something he could be when he was older. How could children be wise? That was silly.

The next day during break Mark overheard Harry Mason teasing the new boy in their class and challenging him to a fight. Harry Mason was the biggest boy in the class. He had spiky black hair which made him look like Denis the Menace.

'Hey, don't be stupid, Mase,' said Mark. 'You're twice his size. Leave him alone.'

Harry turned to Mark. 'Oh, you're going to take his side, are you? Maybe you'd like to fight me in his place?' He towered over Mark, flexing his muscles mockingly.

It wouldn't be the first time Mark had scrapped with Harry but he always came off worst. 'No,' he said. 'I'm not fighting you now. Listen, I thought you wanted some new blood in your football team?'

'Yeah. So what?' said Harry.

'I hear this kid was something of a phenomenon at his old school.'

Harry turned to the new boy, his eyebrows raised. 'Is that right? Okay. Come to practice tomorrow after school. Show us what you can do.'

Mrs Kent, the playground assistant, stopped Mark as he wandered back towards his classroom.

'I saw what happened out there, Mark. Very wise of you.'

Mark stared after her. Him wise? Anyone would be wise not to fight with Harry Mason.

Funny. Now that he thought about it more, he remembered his Dad saying last week that he had made a wise decision. That was when he'd got all his homework done on Friday evening so that he had the weekend free. But that was a very small wisdom.

Mark smiled. If he was wise in small things now, maybe he would be wise in bigger things when he was older. It was just a matter of thinking through your actions and seeing their outcome. Of seeing what would be best for all concerned in the end.

Harry Mason was coming towards him, a big grin on his face and his hair like a jagged halo round his head. But he was no angel. He always seemed to be in trouble one way or the other. Perhaps it was because he wasn't very wise in making decisions. Denis the Menace was right.

He grasped Mark's sweater and half lifted him off the ground.

'Hey Mark. What's so funny?'

'Just the pleasure of seeing you, Mase,' said Mark, wisely.

QUESTIONS FOR THINKING

1. Why did Mark think that he couldn't be wise?

2. What did Mark actually say or do to change Harry's mind about fighting? Do you think this was a wise action? Why?

3. Mark thought that if you practised being wise in small things you would learn to be able to be wise in bigger things. Do you think this is true? Have you any evidence?

4. Has anyone an example of being wise? (Take examples)

5. Why do you think that action was wise? What is there about it that makes it wise?

6. On the evidence we've heard, do you think it is possible for each one of us to be wise?

7. What is wisdom?

8. What is knowledge?

9. Are wisdom and knowledge the same?

10. Is it possible to be wise in the future? Is it possible to be wise in the past? When is it possible to be wise?

Thought for the Week

We can all be wise in our actions by making good choices when we are involved in everyday situations. The only way to do that is by being awake and aware at the time, and realising what the consequences of our actions will be.

Block 2 • Session 6

'Treasures of a Wise Man' Teaching Notes

1. Practise the focusing exercise, directing children's attention to the sense of sight. Remind them that in doing this practice of being in the present, things seen should not be named - just seen and known.

2. Recall the 'Thought for the Week', and discuss any new evidence that has been observed.

3. Read the poem 'Treasures of a Wise Man', then give out copies and allow children to read it to themselves. They should then read it to a partner, each trying to listen to the sound of the voice speaking. This may be a new experience for some, but will allow the meaning to be shown. (It is another way of focusing attention).

4. Give children a copy each. Working in pairs let each child read one of the parts so that the poem forms a conversation.

5. Moving to consideration of theme, give pupils time to consider possible themes and their reasons for choosing the one they chose. The themes and reasons should be shared with a partner.

6. As a class, build up a number of themes on the board and draw links between similar and opposing ideas.

7. Move from the themes on the board to the theme identified in the 'Questions for Thinking' and begin the dialogue.

8. Close by asking children to consider what for them was the most important idea to emerge in the dialogue.

9. Ensure children understand the 'Thought for the Week'.

The Treasures of a Wise Man

Oh, the night was dark and the night was late,
And the robbers came to rob him;
And they picked the locks of his palace gate,
The robbers that came to rob him -
They picked the locks of his palace gate,
Seized his jewels and gems of state,
His coffers of gold and his priceless plate -
The robbers that came to rob him.

But loud laughed he in the morning red!
For of what had the robbers robbed him?
Ho! Hidden safe, as he slept in bed,
When the robbers came to rob him,
They robbed him not of a golden shred
Of the pleasant dreams in his wise old head -
'And they're welcome to all things else,' he said,
When the robbers came to rob him.

James Whitcomb Riley
Bobbs Merrill Fourth Reader(1929)

QUESTIONS FOR THINKING

1. From the poem, can you tell what the wise old man was really?

2. If he was a king or prince he probably had a lot of things to lose. Why did he laugh in the morning?

3. What are possessions? What are yours? What were the old man's?

4. Are your possessions part of you? What are they?

5. How would you feel if your possessions were stolen? Why?

6. What did the wise man value?

7. Do you think it was wise of him not to mind when his possessions were stolen? Why or why not?

8. If you didn't have your possessions would you still be the same person?

9. If you had different possessions would you be the same person?

Thought for the Week

Remember the poem during the week and consider what for you is most important. Is it your possessions, or is it something else? Why - what makes it important?

Block 2 • Session 7

'The Three Axes' Teaching Notes

1. Practise the calming exercise.

2. Remember the poem about the wise man's treasures, and get someone to read it again. Did anyone observe what it is that they hold dear - what is important to them. Take examples and discuss.

3. Read the story 'The Three Axes'.

4. Continuing to reinforce the work on content and theme, ask children to think of two questions relating to the content of the story. Today let these be addressed to the class, so that half a dozen pupils have the opportunity to ask questions.

5. Moving to the theme, give pupils time to consider what for them is the main theme. After sharing theme and reasoning with a partner, each pair should join with another pair to make a small group. Each person should then give their theme and reasons for their choice. The group should discuss these, then choose a group theme from those discussed.

6. On the board a list of the group themes should be built up, drawing links as in past weeks.

7. Move to the dialogue through using the 'Questions for Thinking' to begin the process.

8. Ensure children understand the 'Thought for the Week', and what they should do.

THE THREE AXES

Rama walked home slowly through the woods. Every so often he would stop for a rest and lay the weight of his axe on the ground. He was tired after a long day chopping wood.

He came to the river and walked along its banks. There was a cool breeze which ruffled his hair and some ducks squabbled as they bobbed on the water.

Rama was a poor man but he was happy. He had a wife called Veena and soon there was to be a child.

As Rama walked he thought of his wife who would be waiting for him in their small cottage, with a meal and a loving welcome. Suddenly he tripped over a root and lost his grip on the axe. It hurtled into the river and vanished into the deep water.

Rama didn't know what to do. It had been his only axe. How could he earn his living now? He sat down on the river bank with his head in his hands in despair. He had no money to buy another axe.

Then, from out of the water, came the river goddess.

'What is the matter, Rama?' she asked.

When he told her she dived into the water and brought up a golden axe.

'Is this your axe?' she asked.

'No,' said Rama.

The goddess dived in again and brought up a silver axe.

'Is this your axe?' she asked.

'No,' said Rama again.

For the third time she dived in and this time brought up Rama's axe.

'Is this your axe?' she asked.

Rama smiled and nodded. 'Yes, that is my axe. Thank you very much.'

The river goddess smiled. 'You are so honest,' she said, 'that you have earned all three axes.'

Rama went home with the three axes, knowing that he would never be poor again. He told his wife about it and he told his neighbours. He told his friends and everyone he knew.

But a greedy man heard the story and went and dropped his axe into the river on purpose.

When the river goddess brought up the golden axe the man lied and said that it was his. This made the river goddess angry.

'You are dishonest and greedy!' she said. 'You shan't have any axe.'

And the greedy man had to go home without his axe and no way to earn his living.

QUESTIONS FOR THINKING

1. Why do you think this story was first told?

2. What do people mean by the saying 'Honesty is the best policy'?

3. Do you think it is the best policy? Why?

4. Are you honest? Why? What makes you honest (if you are)?

5. Are you ever dishonest? Why?

6. Is it ever right to be dishonest?

7. Does it matter whether we are honest or not? How?

8. What would this school be like if everyone was dishonest?

9. What would it be like if everyone was honest?

Thought for the Week

Watch your actions during the week and see if you are honest in dealing with other people. Try to look for consequences of being honest or dishonest.

Block 2 • Session 8

'Cinderella' Teaching Notes

Before the lesson, copy a set of 'Character Cards' and a set of 'Statements' for each group of four or five pupils. Cut them out and put into envelopes, one per group.

1. Practise the calming exercise. Ask children what they noticed going on in their mind, for example, did they drift off into daydreams for long periods or were they able to stay quite focused?

2. Remember the story 'The Three Axes', and enquire as to what has been observed about honesty and honest action.

3. Remind the children what happens in a Critical Challenge, and read them 'Cinderella'.

4. The first pupil task is to match the statements with the characters, and they can only do this when the whole group agrees on where it should be placed. This is to facilitate dialogue. Give 10 or 15 minutes for this, as is necessary.

5. Move around the groups, scaffolding their thinking if necessary, unless you are formatively assessing one group using the Criterion - referenced Matrix.

6. Ask each group to report back on **one** of the characters, giving the statements they think should be attributed to that character, and their reasons for thinking so. The next group takes the next character, and so on. Remember to remind pupils that they can challenge weak evidence in the same way as previously.

7. The Critical Question: Is there any theme or 'moral' to the story, and if so, what is it?

CINDERELLA

Once upon a time there lived an unhappy young girl. She was unhappy because her mother was dead and her father had married another woman, a widow with two daughters. Her stepmother didn't like her one bit and although she fussed over her own daughters and was always spoiling them with presents, all that Ella got was old clothes and harsh words. She had to work hard all day keeping the cottage clean and tidy, and all she got by way of rest was the chance to sit for a time by the fire each evening. For this reason she got her nickname 'Cinders', or 'Cinderella'.

One night as she sat all alone by the fire, (everyone else having gone to bed), something amazing happened - there was a burst of light and a fairy appeared. Now you may not believe in fairies, but I can tell you that neither did Ella until that night!

'Don't be scared Cinderella,' said the fairy, 'I caught your thoughts on the wind and I know you would like to go to the Prince's Ball, and so you shall!'

'But look at me - dressed in rags! How can I go to the ball like this?' said Cinderella.

The fairy smiled. 'Have faith,' she said. 'Bring me a large pumpkin and seven mice.' Dutifully, Cinderella set about finding what the fairy wanted. From the basement she brought seven mice that had been busy nibbling the flour sack, then she returned for a large pumpkin from the pantry. With a wave of her wand Cinderella's rags were turned into a beautiful ball gown, and on her head was set a lovely sparkling tiara. Cinderella gasped as she caught sight of herself in the mirror. The fairy carried the pumpkin outside and the mice dutifully followed her, just like trained pets. With another wave of her wand the pumpkin was transformed into a sparkling carriage and the mice were turned into six fine horses and a footman to drive them. Cinderella could hardly believe her eyes!

'Now my dear,' said the fairy, 'go to the ball and have a wonderful time, but remember the magic only lasts until midnight so you must be home by then!'

As Cinderella entered the ballroom a hush fell over the room. Everyone stopped to admire her elegance, her beauty, and the graceful way in which she moved. 'Who is she?' everyone whispered, 'she's gorgeous!' Of course the prince also noticed her, and was quick to go across the room to welcome her. Bowing deeply the prince asked Cinderella to dance, and much to the annoyance of all the other young ladies present, he danced the whole evening with her. Of course the prince was keen to discover just who she was, but despite his repeated questions, Cinderella remained silent about her name and where she came from. 'Let's just enjoy being together, because this is the only time it will happen,' she said.

Cinderella had a wonderful time, quite beyond her dreams, but all of a sudden she heard the sound of a clock striking the hour - the first stroke of midnight! Without time to say goodbye, Cinderella slipped from the arm of the prince and ran across the room and down the large steps leading to the driveway, where the horses and carriages stood waiting. Such was her hurry that as she ran she lost one of her shoes and didn't even have time to stop to get it. The prince, who was now madly in love with Cinderella, quickly followed her outside and down the steps, finding the shoe as he went. As Cinderella disappeared into the night he turned to his ministers and said, 'Go and search everywhere for the girl whose foot fits this shoe. I will not rest until the girl is found.'

This is absolutely amazing. Nothing like this has happened to me before.	I don't understand what's happening to me - this is unreal.
Thank you for a wonderful evening.	I wonder who she is, she is beautiful.
They make such a lovely couple.	This is a wonderful occasion - we're all so lucky to have been invited.
You're a lazy good-for-nothing. I don't know why we keep you.	Goodness always leads to happiness.
These girls are bound to meet handsome young men who will want to marry them.	I can pick up your thoughts.
I only wanted to get married to have some security - a roof over our heads!	Negative thoughts always lead to unhappiness.
'You should always look after 'number one', look after yourself first, that's what I say.'	In life, we all get what we deserve.
I want you to find the person who owns this shoe.	Who are you and where do you come from?
Being wealthy doesn't lead to happiness.	I want happiness more than anything else.
I would like to help you but I don't want to cause trouble.	Without her my life will not be complete.
We're liked more than you.	You know I still love you, you will be happy again.
I don't know what he sees in her - he hasn't danced with either of us, yet.	Life was difficult for me without a wife.

Cinderella	Prince
Stepmother	Father
People at the Ball	Stepsisters

Block 2 • Session 9

'Douglas Bader' Teaching Notes

1. Practise the exercise, asking pupils what they observed about the sense of touch. The important thing is not to list the things realised through touch, but rather that one can be brought into the present moment through touch.

2. Introduce and read the story 'Douglas Bader'.

3. As in previous weeks, ask the pupils to consider an important theme in the story, and why they think it is so. Give time.

4. Working in small groups of four or five, children should discuss the identified themes and choose the one they think is the strongest.

5. Briefly returning to work as a class, review the nature of philosophical questions.

6. Working with their group theme, each group should now turn it into a philosophical question. After a suitable time, these should be written on the board. If necessary, groups can give any explanation of their choice.

7. Making a link between questions on the board (and possibly using an appropriate one to begin) use the 'Questions for Thinking' to stimulate dialogue.

8. To close, connect the questions on the board, and what has been covered through the enquiry.

9. Introduce the 'Thought for the Week'.

DOUGLAS BADER

WW2 RAF Hero

Douglas scanned the skies around him. Suddenly he could no longer see the rest of his squadron. He was alone in his Spitfire over occupied France, and in the distance six German Messerschmidts hurtled towards him.

Douglas shifted in his cramped seat to find a more comfortable position and straightened his artificial legs. Now he was ready to do battle. He throttled back and soared in a wide arc, got one of the German planes in his sights and fired. A hit! Then he rounded on a second one and shot that one down.

But his luck was running out. One fighter against six are impossible odds. He did manage to cripple a third but on its way down it ploughed into his small plane, tearing it in two.

Douglas pulled the little rubber ball above his head which jettisoned the cockpit canopy and the wind roared in his ears as he pulled the harness pin to release himself. Then there was a tremendous noise and buffeting and he was sucked out as though by a large vacuum cleaner, his helmet and goggles wrenched from his head. But he couldn't get clear. What was wrong? He looked down and saw that his right leg was caught. Hanging upside down, he struggled to release his tin leg. The ground was terrifyingly close. He could see a man in a blue smock with a yoke on his shoulders, carrying two buckets. A woman with a scarf was with him. Both were looking up, shading their eyes with a hand, watching him. Then there was a snapping sound and suddenly he was free. He pulled the rip cord on his parachute. For a moment nothing happened, then he felt a tug as the parachute flared open above him like a giant mushroom. Douglas grinned. His luck hadn't run out yet.

He made a hard and undignified landing with his one artificial leg and lay for a moment winded and hurting all over.

When he finally opened his eyes and looked up it was into the faces of two German soldiers.

A stretcher was brought and he was taken by ambulance to a military hospital under German guard. He was not badly injured but couldn't walk with only one artificial leg so the German officials, in an act of respect and courtesy, radioed the RAF and allowed a British fighter to parachute a new leg for him.

That was their big mistake. Within 48 hours, Douglas had knotted his sheets together and was clambering out of the window of the hospital in the first of his many escapes.

QUESTIONS FOR THINKING

1. How do you think Douglas felt when his leg was trapped?

2. What did he do?

3. What clues do we get from the text about the character of Douglas Bader?

4. What are other qualities that people can have?

5. What (positive) qualities do you see in people in this class?

6. What do you think are your own qualities?

7. There is a saying 'If at first you don't succeed, try, try, and try again'. Is this wise? Why? (Why not?)

8. Is it wise to be determined, to persevere? Why?

9. Is it ever not wise (to persevere)?

Thought for the Week

Observe your thoughts and actions during the week. Do you have a positive attitude? Do you persevere to successfully complete things?

Block 2 • Session 10

'Art or Vandalism' Teaching Notes

1. Do the calming exercise. Ask the children for observations on what was experienced. Try to determine if they are aware of the focus of their attention. The aim is to be aware of the present moment.

2. Recall the 'Thought for the Week' from last week, and seek observations on perseverance and a positive attitude. What have pupils noticed?

3. Tell the class that this week they are going to use a newspaper as a stimulus. Read 'Art or Violence?'

4. Ask the class what they think is the main theme of the article. Give time for this, then ask them to turn the theme into a philosophical question. Again, give adequate time.

5. Working in groups of four or five, pupils should share their questions, then decide on which is the strongest, which will be their group question. If necessary, the group can take a vote in order to find the question.

6. As a class, the groups report back, giving their question and reasoning. The questions should be listed on the board. The class now vote on the question they would most like to explore through enquiry. The person who thought of that question begins the dialogue by stating the question then giving their viewpoint and reasoning.

7. Teachers, if necessary refer to the types of questions in the section headed 'Creating Good Dialogue Through Questioning' at the beginning of the book.

8. If the natural dialogue comes to an end, move to the next favourite question on the board.

9. To close, let the class give suggestions for their own 'Thought for the Week.'

ART OR VANDALISM?

by Grant Edwards

Police are cracking down on graffiti artists who deface public or private property.

Despite some graffiti being very artistic, it is a criminal offence, except in designated areas, and offenders can be fined.

All graffiti artists - or writers, as they like to be known - have their own distinctive tag, like a signature, which identifies them. Like all artists, they sign their work so that they get the credit.

But it is these very signatures which have led to several arrests being made. Police believe that people will practise their tags in their school books and are asking teachers to look out for them. Pictures of the tags have been sent to schools to be put up in staff rooms.

Graffiti is nothing new. It was first discovered on ancient Roman architecture. The word 'graffiti' comes from the Greek word, 'graphein' which means 'to write'.

It is, however, on the increase, and now found almost everywhere. Can it enhance an old brick wall or is it just vandalising other people's property?

BLOCK THREE

In this block, the following thinking skills have a particular focus in the pair/group work:

Examining the meaning of the story through language.

The importance of speaking and listening in the learning process, will be emphasised.

Block 3 • Session 1

'The Masks of Life' Teaching Notes

1. Remind children of the two-fold importance of 'the exercise', that is, for the psychological harmonisation (calming effects) of the body, and for learning to 'be in the present'. The latter helps develop meta-cognition - knowledge and insight into one's own thinking - which naturally follows when one is present. Practise the exercise together.

2. Remind pupils of the importance of reflecting on each week's dialogue and keeping in mind the 'Thought for the Week'. Important insights and evidence can become apparent at any time.

3. Read the story 'The Masks of Life'.

4. The pairs work is to examine the meaning of the story through language. This will be a major emphasis for this term. The importance of speaking and listening, in the learning process, should be emphasised to children. The first person should tell the second person what they think the story is saying - its meaning. This can include both literal and 'inner' meaning (that related to theme or philosophical point). When this has finished, the second person **evaluates** what has been said, and gives their own opinion. For example, 'I agree with you about . . . but I disagree that . . . I think . . .' This process should be fully understood by children **before** they begin.

5. Take two or three examples from pupils, then bridge from an appropriate idea to using the 'Questions for Thinking' for the dialogue.

6. Ensure children understand the 'Thought for the Week'.

John loved acting - using different masks and playing different characters. Through his acting, John came to learn more about himself, and to see that all of life is about playing parts. As one wise man said, 'We should learn to play our parts, and play them nicely'.

THE MASKS OF LIFE

John loved acting. Whenever his school were putting on a play or concert, he was the first to volunteer.

For his seventh birthday his Gran and Grandad bought him a set of masks. There was a happy one with a smiling mouth and sparkly eyes and a sad one with a droopy mouth and tears falling from the eyes. There was an angry one with frowning eyebrows, glaring eyes and a thin, straight mouth and an excited one with a huge grin, raised eyebrows and big round eyes.

John played with them for hours. Sometimes he played the happy boy who had just been given an ice-cream and he went round being pleasant and nice to everyone and even offered a pretend lick to his baby sister, who didn't understand about pretend things and cried.

Other times he was the sad boy whose pet hamster had died and he mopped his tears with a tissue and hung his head. Then everyone was expected to pat his head and say how sorry they were.

Or he wore the angry mask of the boy whose friends had all gone to a football match and he wasn't allowed to go. Then he stomped round, shouting and waving his fists until he frightened his little sister.

Another time he would wear the excited mask and play the part of a boy who had just been offered a big part in a film. Then he jumped up and punched the air and laughed hysterically.

One day, near the end of the summer term, John came home from school smiling. 'You look as though you have the happy mask on today, John,' said Mum.
John nodded. 'I really am happy today,' he said. 'Mrs Laird was really pleased with my project about the history of our town and read it out to the class.'

'Well done,' said Mum.

A few days later he came home and slumped into a chair in the kitchen and propped his chin in his hands on the table.

'Hello,' said Mum. 'Today your face looks like the sad mask.'

'I really am sad,' said John. 'I'm not playing. Mrs Laird is leaving at the end of term and I really like her.'

'Never mind,' said Mum. 'I'm sure your new teacher will be very nice.'

Later that evening when John came in from visiting his friend Rob, he went upstairs to play with his masks but soon came down again, scowling.

'Where is my angry mask?' he asked.

'You look as though you're wearing it,' said Dad.

John shook his head in annoyance and stomped into the kitchen. Then he let out a shriek. When he reappeared at the living room door he was holding up the mask, in two pieces. He was breathing quickly and his eyes were cold slits.

'Look what Emily has done!' he yelled. 'She's torn my mask in two!'

'I don't think you need that mask,' said Dad. 'Your face now is much angrier.'

'You shouldn't have left your mask where she could get it,' said Mum.

On the last day of term before the summer holidays, Gran and Grandad came round. They said they had a special surprise for John.

'What is it? What is it?' asked John, jumping up and down and tugging at Gran's arm.

'Grandad and I are going to take you to Disneyland,' said Gran.

John let out a whoop of joy and then laughed and punched the air.

'Ye-e-e-es!' he shouted.

'You look as though you're wearing your excited mask,' said Grandad.

'I'm not playing,' said John. 'I really am excited!'

The day before his trip, John was sitting quietly on his bed watching his mother pack his case. He held his masks in his hands and was looking at each one, even the angry mask, mended with sellotape.

'Who am I really, Mum?' he asked.

His mum stopped packing and looked up.

'You remember when you were happy when your work was praised at school and then sad because your favourite teacher was leaving?'

John nodded.

'You remember how you were angry when Emily tore your mask and excited when Gran and Grandad told you about the trip to Disneyland?'

John nodded again.

'Each of these times,' said Mum, 'we told you that you reminded us of your masks. You John, the real you, is Spirit, watching all that goes on. What you see are all the parts you play, the masks you have to play with. You can put any of them on at any time, in fact, you can choose which to put on and which parts to play. Happy, sad, angry, excited - anything.'

All the world's a stage,
And all the men and women merely players;
They all have their exits and their entrances,
And one man in his time plays many parts . . .
As You Like It *Act II, Scene 7*
Shakespeare

QUESTIONS FOR THINKING

1. All of us have had times when we have felt happy or sad, excited or angry. We put on our different faces. What have you noticed goes with a change of face? (A change of emotion, feeling, the feeling matches the face, etc).

2. Why do we put on different faces? What are the causes?

3. Why did John's Mum say he didn't need to take his masks on holiday with him?

4. Is there ever a right time to put on a mask (face)?

5. If John chose to take his 'happy face' on holiday with Gran and Grandad, what do you think the consequences would have been? See if you can get at least two. (He would look happy, he would feel happy, probably his Gran and Grandad would feel happy, other people would be affected by his happiness).

6. Is it possible to choose the happy mask all the time? Why or why not?

7. If you see the cause of putting on one face or another, do you have the choice to change it? Discuss.

8. What do you think the first two lines of the quotation from Shakespeare mean?

Thought for the Week

See if you can notice what sorts of masks you put on during the week, and also see how you feel at that time.

Block 3 • Session 2

'Anger' Teaching Notes

1. Practise the exercise, and praise the children who were obviously connected to the present moment.

2. What have children noticed about violence, either in themselves or in others. Was anything learnt about how it could be changed?

3. Read the poem and ask children to focus on the **sound** of your voice.

4. Let each child have sight of a copy of the poem, and working in pairs, read it aloud to their partner.

5. Discuss the fact that a child wrote the poem and ask some questions about the content and the language.

6. Use the 'Questions for Thinking' to stimulate the dialogue.

7. To close the session, ask pupils what, for them, was a new idea they have heard today.

8. Discuss the 'Thought for the Week'.

Anger

I was angry and mad,
And it seemed that there was hot water inside me,
As I got madder and madder,
The water got hotter and hotter all the time,
I was in a rage,
Then I began to see colours,
Like black and red,
Then as I got madder and madder,
My eyes began to pop out of my head,
They were popping up and down,
It was horrible,
And it would not stop,
I was steaming with anger,
Nobody could stop me,
My mother could not stop me,
Then it was gone,
And I was alright,
Horrible, black, madness.

Yvonne Lowe
(Aged 8)

QUESTIONS FOR THINKING

1. Look at how Yvonne felt when she was angry. Have you ever had similar feelings? (Take some descriptions).

2. What makes people angry?

3. What makes you angry?

4. Suddenly, Yvonne seemed to feel alright, the anger had gone. If you get angry, does your anger just go suddenly?

5. Do you think Yvonne was happy when she was mad? Have you any evidence?

6. Why do we get angry? Have you a choice?

7. What exactly is anger? Can you describe it or give a definition?

8. What are the results of anger? (Not just in the person getting angry).

Thought for the Week

Observe your own behaviour during the week. Watch to see if you get angry, and if you can see the cause. Can you choose not to be angry?

117

Block 3 • Session 3

'Paul's Boat' Teaching Notes

1. Practise the focusing exercise, in particular drawing children's attention to the importance of listening.

2. Recall last week's 'Thought for the Week' and see what children have observed about anger, and also about the possibility of controlling it.

3. Read 'Paul's Boat', then practise again the examination of the meaning through articulating it - as in Session 1. If possible, children who did not have first turn in session 1 should do so today. They explain what they understand the meaning of the story to be, then the second person evaluates and replies. Remind children of any appropriate protocols such as 'I disagree with you about . . . because . . . I think . . .' (For use as appropriate).

4. Hear two or three examples from children, then bridge from an appropriate one to the 'Questions for Thinking' to stimulate the dialogue.

5. Ensure children understand the 'Thought for the Week'.

In a world of quick fixes and instant solutions, patience is sometimes needed to see a task through to conclusion. This is an important attitude to develop, as it affects an individual's approach to, and success in, life. Those who give in at the first hurdle to any problem have the idea of failure reinforced, leading to low self-esteem. Such individuals avoid challenging situations. Conversely, just having the idea of patiently persevering with something, leads to more success, higher self-esteem and a generally more positive cycle.

PAUL'S BOAT

Paul loved boats but the only one he had been on was the ferry going to France. He dreamed of joining the Merchant Navy or sailing single handed round the world. He wished he had been a sailor long ago in those great wooden sailing ships exploring all corners of the world. He pictured himself climbing the rigging to furl the sails, the ship tossing beneath him, salty spray in his face.

Now the first step in this dream had happened. He and his family had moved into a house with a river running behind. It wasn't a major river, in fact it was only about five metres wide and one deep, just a tributary really. But it was a start.

Now he had decided to build a boat so he could sail on the river. He couldn't wait. They'd hardly been in the new house a week and Paul was out looking for pieces of wood suitable for his boat. He'd seen some discarded planks on some waste ground. He'd have the boat built in no time. It shouldn't be difficult, after all, wood floated.

All Saturday he worked. He drew a simple design for a dinghy and rummaged in his Dad's garage for a saw, hammer and nails. Soon he'd be sailing on the river, exploring as far as he could. He'd give the boat a name and might even put a mast and sails on it to catch the wind. Ah - he mustn't forget some oars to begin with. There was still another week left of the summer holidays. Plenty of time. For the next two days he sawed and hammered. Sometimes his Mum or Dad or older brother Robin came to look. 'How's it going, son?' his Dad would ask. Robin had no interest in boats and just laughed.

By the third day Paul had to admit that it didn't look much like a boat. The bits of wood were all different lengths and thicknesses and were not curved of course. Even as just a square raft with sides it looked odd and he was afraid to try it out to see if it floated. Besides, he didn't want a raft, he wanted a boat.

He sat glumly, head in hands, staring at the silly contraption he'd built. Some of the nails were too long too, and protruded dangerously through the wood. Paul got up, wandered down to the river and squatted at the water's edge staring into it. He'd really expected to be sailing on it by now. 'Not working on the boat, son?' It was his Dad, who'd come up behind him. Paul shook his head. 'It's no good,' he said. 'It's silly.'

'Well, you tried,' said his Dad. 'But to do anything properly you need the right material. Boat-building is a skilled craft, not just a matter of nailing a few bits of wood together.' Paul nodded.

'Don't give up,' said Dad. 'Just wait. Have patience and I'll see what I can do. But it won't be finished before the end of the holidays. You know what I've always said - if you're going to do a job, do it properly.'

A few days later Paul's Dad brought home a roll of thick paper and handed it to him. It was the plans for a boat. Proper plans! Paul studied it carefully. It was very detailed showing all the measurements and required pieces of wood, even the type of wood.

Paul began the autumn term at his new school and made some friends, even one who was also keen on sailing and offered to help with the boat-building.

His Dad bought the timber and other materials needed and agreed to leave the car out in the drive so that the boat could be built in the garage.

First they built the frame. Then the sides. The cracks between the pieces had to be sealed with special stuff to make them water-tight. Then they put in the seats.

Christmas came and Paul got a pair of oars as a present. Still the boat-building went on. Finally, by March, there was only the varnishing to do, and another important feature. Her name. Paul racked his brains for something appropriate. 'Well,' said Mum, coming to inspect the boat. 'You thought you could build a boat in a couple of days but it's taken six months. All your patience and hard work have been worth it, haven't they?' She smiled at Paul.

'That's it!' said Paul. 'I'll call her Patience!' Dad nodded. 'A good name too,' he said. 'Many famous ships had similar sorts of names. Just think of Captain Cook's Endeavour and Resolution and Nelson's Victory.'

'Can we launch her too, Dad, like a real ship?'

'Yes, but not with champagne. We don't want all that broken glass in the river,' said Dad with a smile.

So they painted Patience on her bow and gave her three coats of special varnish.

At last she was finished and Paul stood back and looked at the boat with pride. He and his friend Rick and Robin and Dad carried the boat down to the river for the launching.

It had taken a long time, but when Paul thought back to his first efforts at boat-building he smiled to himself. How silly he'd been. How impatient. This had all been worth waiting for.

QUESTIONS FOR THINKING

1. What was the motivating idea that started Paul building a boat?

2. Can you describe his feelings (emotions) at the start, which made him want to get started straight away?

3. What do you think Paul's Dad thought about the first boat?

4. Why do you think he let Paul carry on with the boat?

5. How did Paul feel by the third day - what were his feelings then? What had he realised?

6. Do you think Paul's emotions were different during the building of the second boat to those during the building of the first (as in question 2)? Why? What were his feelings in the end?

7. There is a saying, 'Patience is a virtue'. Why do you think people say this? Is it true? Has anyone any evidence? (Virtue means it has special worth or merit - it is something special and worthwhile).

8. What is patience?

9. What is it that you love in your friends and family? Is it things on the outside or things on the inside, or both? (Get children to explain their answers).

10. What makes us impatient? What makes us patient?

11. Can we choose to be patient? How?

Thought for the Week

Things that are worthwhile often need patience to 'see them through' or complete them successfully. Try to notice the times when you are having patience to complete a task.

Block 3 • Session 4

'The Trip to France' Teaching Notes

1. Ensure that before the session, a copy is made of the True/Not True/Can't Decide sheet for each group of four or five children. The sheet of items for discussion should also be copied on to card for each group, then cut up. The items should be placed in group envelopes.

2. Practise the focusing exercise.

3. Working in groups of four or five, the task is to place the discussion items into one of the boxes – True, Not True, or Can't Decide. It is important that the group **discuss** each item. They must **all** agree, in order for it to be placed in 'True' or 'Not True', otherwise it goes in 'Can't Decide'.

4. After working through all the items, the groups should return to the 'Can't Decide' group and re-work those items. Group members can try to persuade each other through good reasoning, as to where each item should go.

5. After a suitable time, each group should report back on their findings, noting differences and similarities between groups.

6. To conclude, one of the more contentious items should be chosen as the topic for a 10 minute dialogue.

THE TRIP TO FRANCE

Sam and Lee were excited – the trip to France was now only three weeks away. They had heard the stories each year as the 'big ones' came back from the trip, and here they were, the senior class at last!

'Do you want to come in a tent with me, Sam?' asked Lee.

'Yes, but we'll need some more people – Mrs Phelps said you have to have four or five in a tent.' Sam turned to look around the playground. 'What about asking Scott and Brett?' The two friends went off to find others to share their tent.

The trip to Vias, in the South of France, had become a big event in the Holly Primary school year. Miss Betteridge, the Headteacher, began the planning about a year in advance and all the children started paying something towards the cost each week. The class also did fund-raising for all the extra things such as the meals on the way back, and the extra sun cream and first aid that was so important to take. The final meeting of parents had already taken place and the Mums and Dads all had the information about when the coach was leaving, what clothes each person should take, and emergency procedures.

'Yeah, we should have a good chance at getting the prize for most effort if we all really try.' Ross was trying to convince the others to do their best. 'My brother was there two years ago and he said it was fantastic. The windsurfing is amazing and you get to go on your own.'

'There is a safety boat there.' Lee interrupted. 'And you always have to have a BA on.'

'So what – that's only sensible. Adam says it was the best trip he's ever been on – better than the scout camp.'

'What's a BA?' asked Sam.

'A buoyancy aid, stupid.' Brett was about to snigger, but he thought better of it.

'That's the bell. Come on, we've got to talk with Miss Betteridge about the rules of the trip.' Lee was already running as he shouted over his shoulder.

It is important to keep your tent tidy at all times.	If you are nervous about any of the activities you should try to overcome your fear.
It is important to be able to ask for anything you want in French.	You can be more friendly towards the teachers when you are away.
Anyone who feels a bit homesick must be soft.	If you do not like the food you should complain loudly about it.
You should try to be nice to everyone on the trip, even if they are not nice to you.	You must always do as you are told - safety depends on it.
If you have problems it is better to talk to someone about them.	If you run out of money you can always borrow from someone else. You can pay it back when you get home.
You should 'phone home every day.	No one should try to persuade you to take part in activities you do not want to do.
Your parents have paid a lot of money for the trip so you should make sure you enjoy yourself above all else.	If you are a good swimmer it doesn't matter if you wear a buoyancy aid or not.
If there are team games it is important to only choose the strongest people for your team.	At the disco, make sure you don't hang around with people who don't have trendy gear.
In all activities, working together is always the most important thing.	It's okay to be cheeky to the instructors because you won't ever see them again.
On a trip like this it's important to have a good laugh.	Discipline is not important because you're not in school and it should be the same as when you're on holiday.

Can't Decide

Not True

True

Block 3 • Session 5

'The Bear and the Travellers' Teaching Notes

1. When doing the exercise, it is possible to 'watch' thoughts in mind, as well as out through the senses. This 'watching' is from stillpoint and not being 'lost' in ideas/thoughts. This is related to developing the ability to **give** attention.

2. Recall 'Thought for the Week' and discuss anything the children have discovered about patience. Praise any examples that they may detail.

3. Read 'The Bear and the Travellers'. As in earlier sessions, children should now work in pairs to examine the **meaning** of the story - both literal and philosophical. Use the technique practised in earlier sessions, with one person articulating the meaning then the second of the pair evaluating and responding. The importance of this process of articulating aloud in the learning process, cannot be over-emphasised.

4. Hear several children reporting back their opinions and reasons then bridge from a suitable idea to the 'Questions for Thinking' to begin the dialogue.

5. Ensure children understand the 'Thought for the Week'.

THE BEAR AND THE TRAVELLERS

Adapted from an Aesop's Fable

Two men were travelling together through the forest in Finland. They were going fishing in one of the local lakes. It was springtime and the deep frost had now melted, so that Lake Impo was no longer covered with a thick layer of ice.

Kari and Matti had been friends for a long time and often liked to enjoy the outdoors together. There were spring flowers on the forest floor and the birds were singing in the warm sunshine. Despite this, the friends were a little wary. Springtime was also the time when bears came out from hibernation, and after the long winter were hungry and likely to be even more unpredictable than usual.

Carefully placing their feet as they descended the narrow track to the shore, Kari and Matti had become absorbed in conversation about the best kind of fishing bait to use. Suddenly, as they rounded a bend, they were confronted by a large bear. The bear also seemed startled, despite the warning sound of the friends' chatter, and all three stood still, startled, for a moment. With a cry choked by fear, Matti ran to a tree with low-slung branches and began to climb. Stirred into action, the bear also let out a roar and began moving towards Kari. Kari's route to safety was cut off, and he knew he wouldn't make it into the tree before being caught by the angry bear. Kari fell to the ground as if in a faint, and pretended to be dead. As the bear felt him with its snout, although petrified, he held his breath and lay absolutely still.

It is said that a bear will not touch a dead body, and after a little while the bear ambled off making growling noises. When he thought it was safe, Matti climbed out of the tree and joined a shaking Kari, who was still as white as a sheet.

'Hey, that was a lucky escape,' said Matti. 'What was the bear whispering in your ear?' he continued, trying now to make a joke of the incident.
'He gave me this advice,' Kari replied. 'Never travel with a friend who deserts you in time of danger!'

QUESTIONS FOR THINKING

1. Was it fair of Kari to think that Matti had left him to fend for himself?

2. Why do you think Aesop wrote the original tale?

3. What is a friend? Are there different kinds?

4. What is a 'fairweather friend'?

5. What are the qualities of your friends?

6. What qualities do you show as a friend to others?

7. Would anyone describe you as a good friend? Why?

8. Do you choose your friends? How do you choose them?

9. Is it important to choose friends? Why? Why not?

10. There is a saying 'A person is known by the company he/she keeps'. Is this true? What evidence do you have?

Thought for the Week

Be aware of how you interact with your friends. What qualities do you show in your friendship?

Block 3 • Session 6

'My Thoughts' Teaching Notes

1. Practise the focusing exercise.

2. Ask children what they noticed about similarties and differences in people - what was the most important and why?

3. Read 'My Thoughts' then give copies so that children have sight of one. Children should read the poem silently then aloud to a partner, **listening to the sound** of their own voice.

4. Continuing to work in pairs, the pupils should discuss the text, trying to make sense of it.

5. Making groups out of two pairs, each group should discuss what they have found about the meaning, and formulate a group philosophical question.

6. The questions should be written on the board and any links drawn between them. If possible, make connections with the theme followed in the 'Questions for Thinking', then use them to begin the dialogue.

7. Introduce the 'Thought for the Week'.

My Thoughts

I sometimes wonder what my mind is like inside, often I fancy that it is like this. I feel as if my mind goes round and round and round like the earth, and if my lessons make me think hard it begins to spin. In my other class it was getting all stodgy and still and lumpy and rusty. I feel as if there is a ball in my mind and it is divided into pieces – each piece stands for a different mood. This ball turns every now and then and that's what makes me change moods. I have my learning mood, my good looks mood, my happy mood, my loose end mood, and my grumpy mood, my miserable mood, my thoughtful mood and my planning mood. At the moment I am writing this I am in my thoughtful mood. When I am in my thoughtful mood I think out my maths and plan stories and poems. When my kitten is in her thoughtful mood she thinks shall I pounce or not, and shall I go to sleep or not. This sort of thing goes on in my own mind too. It is very hard for me to put my thoughts into words.

Sarah Gristwood

(Aged 7)

QUESTIONS FOR THINKING

1. What does Sarah think her mind is like?

2. What is your mind like?

3. Are moods connected to your mind (as Sarah thought)? How?

4. How do you know what you are thinking?

5. Can you control your thoughts?

6. What are thoughts?

7. Do animals have thoughts? How do you know? Evidence?

8. If animals have thoughts, are they the same as your thoughts? How do you know?

9. Is it possible to 'watch' your thinking? If you can, is it something that is of any use?

Thought for the Week

Try watching your thoughts. What do you mainly think about? Can you control your thoughts?

Block 3 • Session 7

'The Heron and the Crab' Teaching Notes

1. Practise the calming and focusing exercise.

2. What have children noticed about their thoughts during the week? Is it easy or difficult to observe them? Can they be controlled? Why? Why not?

3. Read 'The Heron and the Crab', then arrange the pupils into groups of four or five. In the same manner as the previous pair work, one child should begin to articulate the meaning of the story - what is it saying? Next, the other three briefly say what they agree or disagree with, before the second pupil gives their opinion and reasoning. Again, the other three evaluate, and so the process is repeated until each child has had a turn.

4. Ask each group to choose, through discussion, the opinion and reasoning they enjoyed the most. These should then be reported back to the class, and a list made on the board.

5. Draw everyone's attention to the points on the board, then move to the dialogue through the 'Questions for Thinking'.

6. Ensure children understand the 'Thought for the Week'.

This is another story from the Indian Panchatantra tradition.

THE HERON AND THE CRAB

To the north of India lies the tiny village of Kaveli, and just outside the village is a large pond, fed by a tiny stream. In the summertime the stream dries up, but the pond is deep enough to remain until the next rainy season. The village children love to come to swim and play in the pond, and sometimes the old men of the village are to be found sitting on the banks fishing.

A heron used to live among the reeds at the northern end of the pond, and it too loved to stalk the shallow waters, fishing. This particular heron was a very lazy bird - so lazy that it could hardly be bothered to fish. If it could have got its food in some other easier way, then it would have!

One day the heron decided to devise a plan to get a supply of fish without having to do much work. It stalked up and down, up and down, thinking about how this might be possible and at last it hit upon a plan. The next day the heron went down to the edge of the pond and put on a gloomy face, without attempting to catch any fish. Now the pond was also inhabited by a wise old crab, who would sometimes help the fish - or anyone else. On seeing the gloomy heron, the crab asked her what was the matter.

'Oh, it's terrible', said the heron, 'we're all going to die. A terrible fate awaits us, it's just too terrible.'

'What are you on about,' said the crab, 'what is so terrible? Surely whatever it is can't be that bad.'

'I heard a group of fishermen talking,' continued the heron. 'This pond is going to be drained so it can be turned into a water system to irrigate the fields. All the fish will die - and they are my only source of food, so I'll die too.' The heron stopped to let the crab take in the bad news. 'However, I may be able to help. I know another pond not far from here, where the fish could be safe. If the fish are interested, I can carry a few a day and fly them to safety.'

The crab duly told the fish the bad news, and they were eager to make use of the heron to reach a safer home. Every day some of them volunteered to go with the heron. She took several a day in her beak and flew off happily. However, on reaching a large rock she would drop the fish on to it, then proceed to eat them, one at a time. In this way she was able to get a continuous supply of fish with no effort at all.

As the days went by the crab began to get suspicious, until one day it volunteered to go instead of the fish. 'Let me go and see my friends and stay with them in their new home,' he said to the heron. Off they flew, but as the crab looked down he saw the large rock with all the dried fish bones shining in the sun. He realised at once what the heron had been up to, and was outraged at the deception. In anger he tightened his claws around the neck of the heron, who crashed to the ground, and lay there without moving. The crab slowly made his way back over the hill to the pond, where he told the fish about the heron's lies.

QUESTIONS FOR THINKING

1. Why do you think the fish trusted the heron?

2. Was there any reason they shouldn't have trusted her?

3. Who do you trust, and why do you trust them?

4. What makes you trust someone?

5. Should you trust everyone? Why, or why not?

6. Can you be trusted? Are there any times you could not be trusted?

7. What is trust?

8. Do we trust anything else besides people? What, and why?

9. What would your family be like without trust? What would your school be like without trust? How do you know?

10. Do you think trust is important? Do you think it is only important here, or do you think it is important everywhere? Do you have reasons or evidence for your answer?

Thought for the Week

Look for ways that trust is shown. See who you trust, and why, and whether people can trust you.

Block 3 • Session 8

'The Big Move' Teaching Notes

1. Ensure that before the session, a copy is made of the True / Not True / Can't Decide sheet for each group of four or five children. The sheet of items for discussion should also be copied on to card for each group, then cut up. The items should be placed in group envelopes.

2. Practise the focusing exercise.

3. Working in groups of four or five, the task is to place the discussion items into one of the boxes - True, Not True, or Can't Decide. It is important that the group discuss each item. They must **all** agree, in order for it to be placed in 'True' or 'Not True', otherwise it goes in 'Can't Decide'.

4. After working through all the items, the groups should return to the 'Can't decide' group and re-work those items. Group members can try to persuade each other through good reasoning, as to where each item should go.

5. After a suitable time, each group should report back on their findings, noting differences and similarities between groups.

6. To conclude, one of the more contentious items should be chosen as the topic for a 10 minute dialogue.

THE BIG MOVE

Claire gripped her mother's hand a little more tightly as they walked briskly along the road. It was all her fault! If only her mother hadn't got a new job they wouldn't have had to move and she could have stayed at Bellevue Primary where she had lots of friends. She would never get another friend like Rachael – they'd known each other since they used to go to nursery together, and she had even been on holiday to Italy with Rachael's family. Claire felt tears welling up in her eyes and tried hard to blink them away – she didn't want these other kids seeing her crying, and she certainly didn't want her mother to get angry again, they'd already had rows about the move.

'Come on Claire, stop dawdling along. I've got to get to work after you've been enrolled at Myreford,' said Mrs Bell.

'I'm not feeling well, Mum. I'm scared about going to such a big school. There's five hundred kids at this school so it won't be as nice as Bellevue – we only had two hundred and fifty there.'

'The headteacher seemed really nice. I'm sure you'll quickly make new friends,' said Mrs Bell, herself a bit worried about starting at her new job.

'Yes, but they won't be like Rachael, Mum.' Claire didn't want to tell her mother she would also miss Richard. All her friends had been jealous that Richard liked her – he always picked her to be in his team in P.E.

The school was now in sight and there were quite a few other children around, all heading in the same direction. Some walked purposefully towards the school and some wandered along in two's and three's, not in any hurry at all. A few stared at Claire, but she tried to ignore them.

'That must be the new girl in our class,' she heard someone say. Nine years old had seemed quite old a few weeks ago, but today Claire felt small and frightened, and she just wanted to disappear.

As they entered the school playground the bell began to ring. Somehow, to Claire, it seemed to signal the start of a new part of her life . . .

Claire must be a 'baby' if she was feeling scared.	Claire's mother should have been more considerate, and not moved job.
Claire would never get a friend as good as Rachael, again.	Claire's mother was a bit worried about starting her new job, so nervousness must run in the family.
Most children make friends easily.	It is normal to feel a bit scared of new situations.
Larger schools are always less friendly than small ones.	Children are always curious about new people joining a class.
If you're curious it means you are rude.	The first day at a new school is always awful.
Claire would never trust her mother.	Rachael wouldn't mind Claire leaving because she still had her other friends.
Claire's schoolwork would get worse because she moved schools.	The children at Myreford Primary wouldn't like a new person joining the class.
The children at Bellevue Primary would probably miss Claire.	If Claire's Dad also had a new job, he was probably feeling a bit nervous too.
There is nothing you can do to make the first day at a new school easier.	The nicer Headteachers are usually in charge of smaller schools.
The best thing would be for the Bell family to help and support each other.	We all react differently to scary situations.

Can't Decide	Not True	True

Block 3 • Session 9

'Jenny's Skates' Teaching Notes

1. Practise the calming and focusing exercise.

2. Read 'Jenny's Skates', then arrange the pupils into groups of four or five. In the same manner as previous pair work, one child should begin to articulate the meaning of the story - what is it saying? Next, the other three briefly say what they agree or disagree with, before the second pupil gives their opinion and reasoning. Again, the other three evaluate, and so the process is repeated until each child has had a turn.

3. Ask each group to choose, through discussion, the opinion and reasoning they enjoyed the most. These should then be reported back to the class, and a list made on the board.

4. Draw everyone's attention to the points on the board, then move to the dialogue through the 'Questions for Thinking'.

5. Ensure children understand the 'Thought for the Week'.

JENNY'S SKATES

'Hi Jenny!' said Narinder, grinning. 'I got some ice skates in the holidays. White leather ones. You know the new rink is open? I'm going to learn figure skating.'

Jenny dumped her schoolbag on the floor and sat down. 'I got the new Gary Haines CD,' she said.

'I want to get that CD too.' said Narinder. 'Are you getting some skates?'

Jenny shrugged, trying to look as if she didn't care. 'You can hire them at the rink.'

Narinder pulled a face. 'Yeah, but it's better to have your own, isn't it Con?'

The boy next to her nodded. 'Do you think you'll be getting some, Jen?'

'Yes,' said Jenny, with more conviction than she felt. She really wanted skates. More than anything else in the world. But they were expensive. Jenny loved watching the skating on TV, especially the ice dance. That was the best.

'Let's go on Saturday,' said Conrad. 'Do you think you'll have your skates by then, Jen?'

'Maybe,' said Jenny. She would ask her mum when she got home. To have a pair of skates of her own would be great. Surely mum would see how happy it would make her?

'We're going skating on Saturday,' she announced when she got home. 'The new rink is open.'

'How much is it?' asked her mother.

'Two pounds.'

'What about hiring skates?'

Jenny hesitated. 'I wondered if you'd buy me a pair - now that you're working. All my friends are getting them. Narinder got some during the holidays ...'

'Jennifer, I can't afford it.'

'There might be some second hand ones in the paper,' said Jenny, hopefully.

'When are you getting your skates?' asked Narinder the next day, clattering her chair down off the table as usual.

'Mum's going to look in the paper for some good second hand ones.'

Narinder sniffed.

Conrad came in. He'd brought his skates to school to show everyone. They were made of smooth black leather and the new blades gleamed. He put them on and wobbled about the classroom.

'You'll blunt the blades,' said Narinder. 'I'm not allowed to walk in mine, even with the guards on.'

Conrad wasn't allowed to for long. Mrs Holson came in and told him to take them off immediately.

'Did you find any skates in the paper?' Jenny asked her mum when she got home.

'You'll have to hire some,' said her mother, shaking her head. 'Perhaps you could have some for your birthday if you're still keen. We'll see.'

'Oh Mum!' wailed Jenny. Her birthday wasn't until August. 'It's not fair! I don't want to hire skates! Everyone else has their own.'

'Then you'll not go,' said Mum, 'and that's the end of it.'

Jenny stomped upstairs to her room and slammed the door. She lay down on the bed facing the wall. How could she face her friends on Saturday in hired skates when she'd said she was getting some?

To her relief skates were not mentioned again until Friday at home time.

'We're meeting at the rink at two o'clock,' said Conrad, swinging his bag over his shoulder. 'Don't forget to bring your skates. See yer.'

Jenny tried to tell him. She opened her mouth to say 'I haven't got any skates. I'm not getting any skates,' but Conrad had pushed through the doors and was gone.

She got there early, bought her ticket and went to the skate hire counter, fumbling with her ticket.

'What size?' asked the man.

'Three please.'

'Give us your shoes then.'

Jenny bent to take off her trainers and put them on the counter. The man was scanning the shelves behind him. He shook his head.

'Sorry, no threes left. Must be a popular size. We've got more on order.'

Jenny stared at her trainers on the counter but did not pick them up. How could they run out of skates?

'Hang on,' said the man, turning back to the shelf. 'Here, borrow these. They're second hand ones that we're selling for someone. Twelve quid if you want to buy them, and don't tell anyone I lent them to you.'

Jenny reached for the skates. They were white leather. She ran her thumb carefully across the double blade. Just what she wanted. If only she had twelve pounds.

Then she had an idea. She grabbed the skates with a grateful grin to the man and went to look for her friends.

'Narinder!' breathlessly she caught up with them at the changing room door. 'Narinder, you know that Gary Haines CD? What will you give me for it?'

Narinder turned and looked at her in surprise and then down at the skates in her hand. 'Why? Do you need some money?'

Jenny nodded. 'I need twelve pounds. I've got four from Christmas and Mum's change here that I'll borrow. I still need a fiver.'

'Done,' said Narinder.

Jenny grinned happily as they went to put their skates on. She had her own pair of skates at last! FANTASTIC!

The three friends went skating nearly every Saturday for a while, but then the other two began making excuses not to go. There were other things they wanted to do. Conrad joined the local 'Under Twelves' football team and Narinder had started going into town shopping with her older sister. Jenny still enjoyed skating and had become quite good and there were still people she knew who went, but she decided she didn't want to be an ice dancer after all.

One thing she really would like was a drum kit. There was a girl drummer in Gary Haines' band . . .

145

QUESTIONS FOR THINKING

1. Can you think of a time when you really wanted something but couldn't have it? (Take various examples)

2. Ask two or three children why they wanted the particular thing they did.

3. What does it feel like to really want something?

4. How did you expect to feel once you had it?

5. Did it happen? Did you feel like you expected to? Did the feeling last? How long? A day . . . a week . . . a month . . . forever?

6. Is it wrong to want things (goods, possessions)?

7. Do we want things for different reasons? What reasons?

8. Are some reasons more important than others? Why?

9. Do the more important things make us more happy?

Thought for the Week

It is nice to get things, but getting things doesn't make us happy for very long - we soon want something else. Look to see what it is that makes you really happy.

Block 3 • Session 10

'Cloned Cows' Teaching Notes

1. Do the calming exercise.

2. Discuss what 'day dreaming' is, and whether children had noticed if they were dreaming during exercise. Which seems more real - the dreaming state or the focused one?

3. Explain to the children they are going to use a magazine article as a stimulus this week. They will be trying to identify any philosophical issues in the story, then frame some philosophical questions. Read 'Cloned Cows'.

4. Ask two or three questions to ensure the pupils have understood the content of the story.

5. Discuss the nature of philosophical questions. Get children to spend time on their own, thinking of what they think is a good theme. They should have reasons for their choice.

6. In pairs, children should discuss their theme and discuss together how the themes could be turned into a philosophical question.

7. Each pair should join together with another pair, and through discussion decide on the best (most interesting) question.

8. Write each group's question on the board. Review the range of questions provided and ask the children to consider the question they would most like to investigate through enquiry. Take a vote to determine the chosen question.

9. Ask the person who originally put forward the question to begin the dialogue by restarting their question and putting forward their own view on it.

10. In building the enquiry, remember to use a variety of questions and encourage the children to do the same. Use ideas from 'The Importance of Skilful Questioning' section, if necessary.

11. If the dialogue runs out, move to the second favourite question, and so on.

CLONED COWS

by Geraldine Tucker

The world's first cow clones have been produced in New Zealand to make cheese-making easier and quicker.

There are nine cows in the herd and scientists say that the milk is easier to process and more stable when it is heated.

This follows on from the famous Dolly, the cloned sheep, who was created in Edinburgh in 1997.

What is a clone? It's a living thing made from another living thing, and is an exact replica of the original.

Cloning isn't new. Plants, like potatoes, send out shoots which grow into a new plant. To grow a plant from a cutting is a type of cloning, and identical twins are clones of each other.

Now an American company says it has cloned a human embryo for the first time - in order to research how cloning can be used to treat diseases such as Aids and cancer. The company said it was not done to create another human being.

The idea of cloned humans has caused controversy and new laws are being made to ban it, although cloning for research would still be allowed.

Glossary of Terms

Community of Enquiry:

A group (generally a class) engaged in exploring and developing ideas through 'Socratic' dialogue.

Critical Challenges:

Critical challenges are activities that have been devised to develop a range of thinking skills, constituting critical thinking.

Critical Thinking:

Critical thinking brings together different thinking skills such as information handling, enquiry skills, reasoning, creative thinking, and evaluation. In particular it involves making reasoned judgements about particular situations in specific contexts using the elements described above.

Dialogue:

The 'Socratic' method of questioning, sometimes called dialectic. The art of critical examination into the truth of an opinion or idea. '..an active process of . . . people enquiring about, and learning from, the distinct perspectives of others, where there is a real, and exciting possibility that their own positions will shift as part of the process'. (James Park)

Emotional Intelligence:

'The capacity for recognising our own feelings and those of others, for motivating ourselves, and for managing emotions well in ourselves and in our relationships.' (Daniel Goleman)

Facilitator:

The person leading a 'community of enquiry.' So called, to move away from the traditional idea of teacher being a dispenser of knowledge.

Formative Assessment:

'Formative assessment is when the evidence (collected) is actually used to adapt the teaching work to meet the needs (of the pupils).' (Dylan William) In other words it is not summative, just a collection of results and scores.

Ideas Web:

A collection of ideas put forward by pupils, in this programme usually in relation to a theme or philosophical question. These are written on the board as they are offered, then connected by lines that join those which are related ideas. Ideas which are in opposition to each other may be connected by lines of a different colour. The result is a visual portrayal of the collective ideas of the group.

Mystery:

In this book a mystery is an activity where a short story is used to set up a scenario in which an event (usually including an ethical or moral dilemma) takes place. Working with pieces of evidence that are additionally supplied, the pupils have to explore possible solutions by bringing different thinking skills into play.

Philosophy:

An enquiry into the nature of our being, and the world in which we live. Literally, the love of wisdom.

Philosophical Question:

Philosophical questions are not easily answered from facts, or calculation such as 'What is 7 plus 5?' They are essentially contentious and lead one to further enquiry, hence the need for dialogue in seeking to answer them. Some people argue that any question can be philosophical, for example in the question above one could ask 'What do you mean by seven?' However with primary school children especially, one should apply the rule of 'reasonableness'. Examples of philosophical questions are: 'What is beauty? What makes an action wrong? Do animals have feelings? Examples of questions not normally thought of as philosophical are: What is the capital of New Zealand? Who is the oldest person in your family? In what year were you born?

A useful strategy to help children to frame a philosophical question is to initially talk about themes. Pupils can, on most occasions, readily identify the theme of a story or poem. From there, ask them to consider how to formulate a question from the theme. For example, if the theme of the story has been identified as beauty, philosophical questions that could be posed include 'What is beauty?' 'How do we know when something is beautiful?' 'Are there different kinds of beauty?' In time children will easily move straight to framing questions.

Philosophy with Children:

Also known as Philosophy for Children (P4C)
The method or process of using 'Socratic questioning' to pursue philosophical questions, using different kinds of stimuli. Engaging in a 'community of enquiry'.

Socratic Method:

The method of using dialectic or open-ended questioning to enquire into a philosophical question.

Spiritual Intelligence:

'. . . the intelligence with which we address and solve problems of meaning and value, the intelligence with which we can place our actions and our lives in a wider, richer, meaning –giving context'. (Dr. Danah Zohar)

Thinking Maps:

'Thinking Maps' are also known as model maps, webbing maps, learning maps, and various other names including at least one that is registered copyright! Thinking maps are a guide to our thinking on something, whether to show the development of an idea, as a study guide to a piece of work or for remembering (i.e. putting back together) the course of a dialogue.

Thinking Skills:

Thinking skills are about having different strategies within our thought processes and knowing when to use them, and about being aware of our thinking (meta-cognition) processes. The number of thinking skills can be numerous, but the generally accepted group includes information handling skills, enquiry skills, reasoning skills, creative thinking skills and evaluation skills.

ACKNOWLEDGEMENTS

Thanks to various people and individuals for permission to use material, copyright or otherwise. To Harcourt, Brace and World Inc., for 'Little Girl Be Careful What You Say' from 'The Complete Poems' by Carl Sandburg; to Andre Deutsch for 'I Wake Up' from 'Quick Let's Get Out of Here' by Michael Rosen.

A special thanks to Steve Trickey and Lesley Robertson for contributing to the dialogue on how to best take this work forward.

Acknowledgement is also made to any copyright holder whom the author has been unable to trace despite careful enquiry.

Sapere Aude - 'Dare to know'

The 'Thinking Through Philosophy' series has been the subject of a rigorous study by Dr S. Trickey and Prof. K. Topping at the University of Dundee (Scotland). Its effectiveness has been well documented. For further information and for INSET and training opportunities see the author's website at

www.aude-education.co.uk